Ruth Field is The Grit Doctor. She lives in North London with her husband and twin sons. She is the author of *Run Fat B!tch Run* and *The Run Fat B!tch Run Marathon Plan*, and a columnist for the *Irish Times*.

Also by this author

RUN FAT B!TCH RUN
THE RUN FAT B!TCH RUN
MARATHON PLAN

GET
YOUR
SH!T
TOGETHER

**Your Prescription
for a Simpler Life
or
LIFE IS A GRIT SANDWICH**

RUTH FIELD
AKA
THE GRIT DOCTOR

sphere

SPHERE

First published in Great Britain in 2013 by Sphere

A CIP catalogue record for this book
is available from the British Library.

ISBN 978-0-7515-5049-8

Typeset in Bembo by M Rules
Printed and bound in Great Britain by
Clays Ltd, St Ives plc

Papers used by Sphere are from well-managed forests
and other responsible sources.

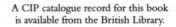
Sphere
An imprint of
Little, Brown Book Group
100 Victoria Embankment
London EC4Y 0DY

An Hachette UK Company
www.hachette.co.uk

www.littlebrown.co.uk

For my grandmother, Patricia Field,
a remarkable woman, who has always
got her s**t together.

ACKNOWLEDGEMENTS

But for the enthusiasm, patience, encouragement and brilliance of my editor – Hannah Boursnell – and my amazing agent – Alice Saunders – I would never have got my shit together. Thank you both for making it all happen. A big thank you to Rhiannon Smith for her technical wizardry and to everyone at Little, Brown and Hachette Ireland for championing The Grit Doctor so enthusiastically.

Heartfelt thanks in no particular order to wonderful friends and contributors: Andrew Breddon, James Stockton, Adam Morane-Griffiths, Anna Field, Tanya Lutyens, Charlotte Pilain, Veronique Mayne, Nicola Helfert, Alice Haddon, Kate Packenham, Nikki Eimer, Josephine O'Riordan, Sara Mackie, Debra Stephens ('eye of the storm'), Clare Daniels, Katkin Taylor, Jacey Topham, Laura Fishbourne, Breda Clifford, Liliana Popovici, Afrim Ponari, and Rasim Dushaj. And to all my family for their support, particularly my dad, for his ever-flowing stream of ideas for The Grit Doctor, and Mum for putting up with all the foul language. I promise *at some stage* to write a book without a swear word in the title. To Lucia Kramlikova – possibly the best child minder in the world – and her brilliant assistants Zanet Misovicova and Anna Tothova, without whom nothing would ever get done. To everyone at Feast Deli in Muswell Hill – I have come to think of Feast as my office and I love coming to work. But, *most importantly*, to my gorgeous husband Olly (a man so devoid of grit and so full of love and goodness) who I have to thank for choosing to share his life – and for laughing at it all – with me.

'Our limbs fail, our senses rot. We degenerate into hideous puppets, haunted by the memory of the passions of which we were too much afraid, and the exquisite temptations that we had not the courage to yield to.' *Oscar Wilde*

CONTENTS

PART 2: INTEGRITY

PART 3: SPIRIT

A WORD OR TWO FROM
THE AUTHOR(S)

ERM, EXCUSE ME, BUT WHO IS
THE GRIT DOCTOR?

For those of you who have read *Run Fat B!tch Run*, The Grit Doctor needs no introduction. For the benefit of you very welcome newcomers, The Grit Doctor is my alter ego, my Inner Bitch – an acid-tongued, arse-whipping taskmistress who helps me get stuff done. Cultivating a strong relationship with your own Inner Bitch is going to be fundamental to your success in the arena of shit togetherness. Don't have one? Yes, you do, she has just been temporarily silenced through lack of use. She is the strict nagging voice in your head who tells you which shit most urgently needs your attention; the voice you usually ignore or try to suffocate with cake or drown out with wine. You need to learn how to coax that voice out of its shell so it can really get in your face, because your Inner Bitch is a veritable maestro of shit togetherness. And fear not, The Grit Doctor will show you how.

The Grit Doctor is not a psychologist, nor is she a real doctor, but she is – without question – the world's leading authority on the subject of grit. Over the years, and most especially since having twin sons two years ago, I have come to realise that grit is at the root of everything I do well and fundamental to my ability to get stuff done – and to get it done fast, which frees up more time to enjoy myself. The application of grit to the task at hand – any task – literally buys me freedom. It is my passport to peace.

The Grit Doctor is all about cutting through unnecessary flab and homing in on what's important. And furthermore, delivering the unpalatable truth with punch and a sense of humour. Because the fact is, we all waste a lot of time doing irrelevant tasks, things that *don't*, in fact, need to be done in order to have our ducks lined up. We all do it. And we get stalled or stuck along the way by playing mind games with ourselves – another huge waste of time. The Grit Doctor abhors these traits and is committed to training you to rid yourself of them.

The good news is that the ability to be gritty is already within you. It is neither a gift nor a talent but a skill that anyone can cultivate.

AND WHO ARE YOU?

I am like you. A working mother of twins, struggling to get my shit together and to make sense of the chaos that seems to dominate my life – probably in much the same way as you are. The only advantage I currently have over you is an incredibly powerful and potent relationship with my Inner Bitch.

ARE YOU *SURE* THIS GRIT STUFF WORKS?

Yes. And I have hundreds of emails and letters from people who read my first book *Run Fat B!tch Run* and embraced The Grit Doctor's philosophy to prove it. Women who had never run further than the bus stop before, but who found their Inner Bitches, gave up their excuses and started putting one foot in front of the other. Some of these women went on to take part in marathons, others have reconnected with their bodies or run their way out of an emotional black hole. I am not going to bang on about running *much* in this book, but I firmly believe that connecting with your Inner Bitch can help you achieve things you thought were impossible, be that running in a race, changing your career or finding the love of your life.

WHAT IS GRIT?

Grit *noun*. firmness of character, indomitable spirit, pluck.

Grit *verb*. clench (the teeth) esp. in order to keep one's resolve when faced with an unpleasant or painful duty.

THE GRIT DOCTOR SAYS:

We are all born plucky.

Over the years our pluck can get buried – by our cynicism, by our disappointments and by our world view. *Our pluck gets stuck.* Think of your pluck or grit as simply another muscle that you were born with. Like all muscles, it needs exercise to take shape and gain strength. Think of it as *gristle*. The more gristle you develop, the easier you are going to find it to power through the boring bits of life admin – *gritmin* – without so much as a second thought – that muscle just gets bigger the more that you put it to use. The big decisions, the huge intimidating tasks – they too can be tackled with verve once your gristle acquires some form.

And here's the thing: there is only one expert who can transform your life. And it is you. What I have to offer you is a first-class education in Grit Management, and by the time you have finished this book and completed the exercises herein you will be able to award yourself a diploma in its dark art. The Grit Doctor will deliver the tutorials in the manner of a slap in the face so that you really 'get it'. If I seem to brush over issues that you consider to be important or appear to be oversimplifying stuff that you always thought of as complex and the territory of experts, *good*. That is precisely the point – simplification is the very DNA of gristle. When I disregard things like our pasts, our childhoods, our emotional issues, even our personalities, this is very deliberate. I am starting from the premise that we are all in essence the same. Another huge time waster and GYST decoy is homing in on all of our differences: gender, race, age, background, job, class – and in so doing creating artificial barriers and obstacles to our progress, to our ability to communicate, to our better under-standing of ourselves and each other. And we lose out hugely as a result.

THE GRIT COMMANDMENTS

Ignore them at your peril.

1. The only expert you need to rely on in your life-long GYST mission is *you*.

2. GYST is a continuing process, not some perfect state that you magically reach.

3. You must have a good sense of humour. Laughing – a lot, and most especially at yourself – is not only essential for your health but is a prerequisite for understanding the contents of this book and embracing its philosophy.

4. The past must remain in the past.

5. You are of sound mental and physical health. If not, see a real doctor who will refer you to a specialist if necessary. If you are overweight and unfit, and can't see the wood for the fat, read *Run Fat B!tch Run* and come back to this book later.

6. You are willing to give yourself over to the care of The Grit Doctor and follow her instructions religiously.

7. You are not expecting to be spoon-fed and are willing to use your own judgement to apply to all tasks and questions. Remember that *you* are the expert and only *you* have the right answers for your life. Start owning it by reacquainting yourself with your basic instinct for sound judgement and common sense.

8. You are not different or special or an exception to the rules. The only exceptions are those expressly stated by The Grit Doctor.

THE GRIT DOCTOR SAYS:

Gritty? You betcha, bitches.

Exercise! THE *TO DON'T* LIST

This is a pointless written declaration that is going to mark the beginning of your shit-togetherness journey. I say pointless because The Grit Doctor is not a fan of lists – they are faffing in disguise. Which is why *this* list is a kind of *un*list and, I hope, one of the last you will *ever* write. The point is for you to have a quick think about your weak points, and the 'reasons' you give for your life not being the way you want it to be. What stops you? What holds you back? What do you always end up doing instead of building those shelves or applying for that job, for example? If you are stuck for ideas, the manner in which you approach this exercise may well reveal quite a few things for your list. If you find yourself wasting hours in search of the Sellotape to attach your list to the fridge, for example, then disorganised/chaotic/messy might be on your list. If you are spending ages decorating your list, perhaps procrastination is a particular weakness of yours? If so, add it to your list. Now. Leave plenty of space at the bottom because as you progress through the book you will uncover many more failings and shortcomings to add onto it. Why are we putting it on the fridge? Because opening the fridge door outside of meal times is a classic displacement activity favoured by many of us and so is a great place to have a decoy. It will serve the dual purpose of preventing us from unnecessary nibbling while hopefully steering us back to the task in hand.

A SAMPLE *TO DON'T* LIST

- Writing lists/decorating lists/P R O C R A S T I N A T I N G

- Opening fridge door to have a look/nibble

- Watching telly mindlessly from the moment I get home from work until midnight

- Moaning

- Slagging people off

- Shopping when skint.

So, your list should by now be written – legibly – and attached to the fridge. Job done. Now is not the time to dwell on just how *un*-GYSTful a state you are in. Acknowledging our weaknesses is the first crucial step towards tackling them and until they are in black and white and in our faces we can continue to pretend they don't exist. So, well done and let's move on.

INTRODUCTION

THE ART OF SHIT
TOGETHERNESS

UP SHIT CREEK

I don't know how she does it.

But does she do it, really? Is her shit *actually* together?

Ms Shit Together	Ms Shit All Over the Place
Ms ST has a handsome husband and two gorgeous well-behaved kids, an immaculate and beautifully designed home, always remembers everyone's birthday and provides thoughtful gifts, hosts amazing dinner parties *and* has a glittering career.	Ms SAOP is single, in a crap job, still sitting on the same uncomfortable futon she had at uni, behind on her council tax and rent, paying for a gym membership she never uses and the most intimate relationship she has is with her remote control.

SO, WHO *REALLY* HAS THEIR SHIT TOGETHER?

Ms Shit Together	Ms Shit All Over the Place
Ms ST spends an hour on a therapist's couch every week moaning that she is unhappy, takes Prozac every night, hasn't had sex with her husband in six months and is paranoid her twenty-three-year-old assistant is trying to steal her job.	Ms SAOP spends every Friday night getting trashed in the pub, complaining to her mates about how crap her life is, and every Saturday morning under the duvet, weeping.

Answer? Neither of them.

The point is that GYST is subjective. That woman at work who you have always envied may not be everything you imagine. Her shit, as the above table illustrates, may in fact be all over the place. Just as that quirky chap you know who lives on a barge and collects vintage teapots may be as GYSTful as is humanly possible. Because once the basics are nailed, GYST is not about *what you have* but about your attitude to life. For most of us, this should come as a huge relief. And, no, it doesn't mean you can sink back into the sofa with the Dairy Milk, close your eyes and tell yourself there is nothing you need to do. There is plenty, it just might not necessarily be what you thought. Read on.

We all have an idea of what getting our shit together feels like, what it looks like, what it is. Who we might be *if only* we had it together. But it isn't so easy to nail down, or to sustain the feeling of having it together for very long. In fact, much like a summer's day in July, it can often feel like a dream we had, so fleetingly does it appear. And, after it's gone, during the days of interminable rain which follow, we remain predominantly in a state of blind panic, overwhelmed by the feeling that we most certainly *do not* have our shit together, that it is, in fact, all over the place . . . and that we look like shit to boot.

And that whole paragraph is just more shit really, isn't it? Unspecific, airy-fairy meaningless rubbish that I have written down to illuminate a critical Grit Doctor principle:

THE GRIT DOCTOR SAYS:

The essence of getting your shit together is BEING
IN ACTION.

GYST ESSENTIALS

In order to even begin to get our shit together, we need to break
it down into something altogether less vague, into something
concrete as opposed to conceptual; into something that we can
nail down rather than something that remains as a figment of our
imagination or, worse still, as a *feeling*. Ideas and feelings are all
well and good, and conceptualising has its place, but the meat and
gravy of getting our shit together lies in doing stuff, in taking specific actions towards completing set tasks, objectives or goals. Our
goals will vary widely but the behaviour necessary to get us there
is the same.

THE GRIT DOCTOR SAYS:

All you need to succeed are a good sense of humour
and a willingness to do as I instruct.

And the beauty of it is, once you develop this skill of **BEING IN ACTION**, the more shit you will get done, and the more that gets done the more you will be inspired to tackle: projects will get bigger and goals higher as you stretch yourself further and begin to realise that you are capable of so much more than you ever gave yourself credit for. And the brilliant thing is that it can be applied to everything that we have going on in our lives that we want to change. It all begins with one step, with one physical action which will encourage another action, and so on and so forth.

'It sounds kind of robotic and boring,' I hear you object. Yes, but you won't be complaining when you are able to apply this simple Grit Doctor principle to getting the job you always dreamed of or getting together with the love of your life.

It will require practice and repetition to coax these new shit-busting skills into a firm habit, but the essence of the thing really is dead simple. Simple in the sense that we can all get our heads round it, we can all do it. In *Run Fat B!tch Run* I wrote about running being a very simple activity. However simple it may be, though, translating that into the act of actually doing it? Not so easy. Not when we have got so stuck in our ways that for the life of us we are unable to detach ourselves from the remote control, stand up, remove our arses upstairs and just build those effing shelves from Ikea which have been lying underneath the bed, gathering dust, since January.

THE GRIT DOCTOR INTERJECTS:

And *this* is where your Inner Bitch comes in. She
is your number one ally in the pursuit of GYST.
She is harsh, even brutal at times, but she is smart
and sassy too. She is the sense of urgency that
quickens your step, she is your conscience, your
better half, your personal trainer, your secretary
and in-built editor. She is the voice that galvanises
your gristle. She is *really* pissed off that you
haven't built those shelves yet. By the time I have
finished with you, you won't be able to ignore
her any longer.

The essential Grit Doctor principle – that action is the key ingredient towards getting our shit together – cannot be overstated.
And action comes first, not last. Not when we have worked
everything out perfectly and when we have all our ducks lined up
and are confident of an assured outcome. Action comes NOW,
at the very beginning, when our shit is still all over the place.
Nothing happens, nothing is achieved, nothing becomes clear,
nothing is even really revealed about who we are *except when we
are in action*. Not convinced? Listen to some leading authorities
on action:

'Action is the foundational key to all success.'
Pablo Picasso

'Action expresses priorities.' *Mahatma Gandhi*

'Human beings must have action; and they will
make it if they cannot find it.' *Albert Einstein*

'An ounce of action is worth a ton of theory.'
Ralph Waldo Emerson

'Inaction breeds doubt and fear. Action breeds
confidence and courage. If you want to conquer
fear, do not sit home and think about it. Go out and
get busy.' *Dale Carnegie*

'Do you want to know who you are? Don't ask.
Act! Action will delineate and define you.'
Thomas Jefferson

'When it is obvious that the goals cannot be
reached, don't adjust the goals, adjust the action
steps.' *Confucius*

'I never worry about action, but only inaction.'
Winston Churchill

'The superior man acts before he speaks, and
afterwards speaks according to his action.'
Confucius

'The time for action is now. It's never
too late to do something.'
Antoine de Saint-Exupéry

'Action is the antidote to despair.' **Joan Baez**

Think of it this way: no amount of talking about it, and thinking about alternative spots to hang it, will get that picture up on
the wall. The only thing that will is deciding where it will go,
getting a hammer out of the tool box, taking out the picture
hook and nailing the effing thing onto the wall. Staring at it on
the floor every night is not an action consistent with realising the
result you desire.* Just as you Run Fat B!tch Runners discovered
that the only way to get fit was to quit bitching and moaning and
get moving, so we will soon discover that the magic in life happens when we are in action. And it *only* happens when we are in
action. Getting into the habit of *doing* things – the physical things
necessary to get stuff done – as and when they arise, and out of
the habit of over-thinking yourself into a stupor and putting things
off until later has to be the answer. If it can be done now, do it
now. It is while in action that your thinking will gain clarity and
it is amazing how much more quickly you can do things than you

---

*An important GD addendum: there's not much in life that, once done, can't be
undone. Murder being an obvious exception. But, as in the more common and realistic example above – if you hate where you've hung the picture, take it down, fill in
the hole and then try somewhere else. Simple.

imagined. Plus, it has a knock-on, domino-type effect in that the more you do, the more you are able to do and the more shit gets done as a result. Easier said than done? Not when you've got your Inner Bitch breathing down your neck 24/7. Trust me.

THE GRIT DOCTOR'S LAWS OF ACTION, WITH THANKS TO ISAAC NEWTON'S LAWS OF MOTION

Isaac Newton devised these three laws of motion over three hundred years ago which form the basis of classical mechanics. They describe the relationship between the forces acting on a body and its subsequent motion. The Grit Doctor has bastardised them to make a point – apologies, Newton.

1. *If an object experiences no net force, then its velocity is constant: the object is either at rest (if its velocity is zero), or it moves in a straight line with constant speed (if its velocity is non-zero).*

THE GRIT DOCTOR SAYS:
Unless you exert force on your lazy motionless ass, your life is never going to change.

---

2. *The acceleration of a body is parallel and directly proportional to the net force acting on the body, is in the direction of the net force, and is inversely proportional to the mass of the body.*

THE GRIT DOCTOR SAYS:

The more grit you are able to unleash, the more bang you will get for your buck.

3. *When a first body exerts a force on a second body, the second body simultaneously exerts a force on the first body.*

THE GRIT DOCTOR SAYS:

Everything you do is action-generating – the more shit you tackle, the more shit you are able to tackle.

YOU are both the object *and* the force.

Even if everything is how you want it to be (extremely unlikely if you are reading this book), you will need to be exerting force somewhere, more or less consistently, just to preserve the status quo. A good life, a really productive life, exists because of all the action that is taken daily to sustain it.

If everything is precisely the way *you don't want it to be*, you need some serious force – rocket fuel – to shift the dynamics of your life. Good news: you have access to force. 24/7. And it is free. The force you have within you that you need to harness in order to become an action-taking aficionado is your Inner Bitch. She is the force. Use the force.

⚡ Exercise! HOW TO LOCATE YOUR INNER BITCH

You are sitting on the sofa – *again* – watching *another* episode of *Come Dine With Me*, which you hate but seem unable to switch off. It is the televisual equivalent of a Big Mac and fries – which you also demolished on your way home from work – an anaesthetic which glues you to your seat. You had a bad day at the office and you feel a mild sense of self-loathing creep over you, but nothing that chocolate and a glug of wine won't help fade into oblivion. You know that now is a perfect opportunity to sort through the pile of bills on the kitchen table and file them away, and you hear a faint little buzzing noise in your ear: Go on, you lazy oaf, sort it out. Another glug of vino, another square of choccy, silences the buzzing.

That mosquito-esque irritant was your Inner Bitch, trying to galvanise you into action.

To find her, I want you to bring to mind someone or something that has incensed you beyond belief. Dwell on it/him/her for a few minutes and indulge in that feeling of simmering rage. See how those nasty, venomous words are springing to your mind quite effortlessly? That is your Inner Bitch. It is very easy to locate her when she is directed against other people, or annoying situations. In the quest for shit togetherness, I want you to turn that sharp-tongued assassin inward, to exert the force necessary to eject you from the sofa and into action.

We *all* have a nasty side, and this is a very good thing. So no more shying away from it or pretending you don't have one. Problems arise when we become overly proficient at directing our nastiness outwards all the time and have lost the ability to put it to much better use – into GYST.

THE GRIT DOCTOR SAYS:

The time has come to quit bitching and moaning about other people's inadequacies and instead unleash that bitch on your own shortcomings.

You need to **start talking to your Inner Bitch to develop your working relationship** by *tuning in* when the buzzing alerts you to her presence rather than trying to tune her *out* all the time. But how? Ask her questions, listen, laugh and obey at the earliest available opportunity.

THE GRIT DOCTOR INTERJECTS:

Be wary of talking to your Inner Bitch in public and running the risk of getting arrested or sectioned. This is a relationship best cultivated in the confines of your own home.

 ## HOW TO RELOCATE A SILENCED INNER BITCH

If you cannot understand what I am talking about and cannot locate your IB, this can only mean that she has been silenced through years of misuse. She is there, I promise you, so do not panic.

Try this visualisation exercise. Close your eyes and call to mind a real-life mega beeeyatch whom you secretly admire: think of a particularly punchy boss from work, or your old PE teacher from school. Or Monica Galetti from *Masterchef*. What would he or she say to you if they saw you slumped on the sofa watching *Come Dine With Me*? (Monica, in particular, would be horrified at the culinary train-smash that characterises the show.) The more you ask an imaginary IB to answer for you in challenging circumstances, the stronger your relationship will become with your own.

I realise that for you Run Fat B!tch Runners, I am trespassing on familiar territory, but you all know how important your Inner

14

Bitch is to your continued success in the area of fitness and health. She is also, unsurprisingly, the key to success in all areas of our lives. She is your own internal shit-togetherness *expert*: the strict voice of reason that we choose to ignore to our detriment, because she makes GYST so much easier. And she is available around the clock to marshal us into action. Remember: she is the force.

The Grit Doctor interrupts these very important IB-locator exercises to remind readers that a sense of humour is vital for the understanding, appreciation and application of any of the exercises and programmes herein. Lose your sense of humour and you lose everything. Period.

THE GRIT DOCTOR WILL SEE YOU NOW

Q: But I don't have an Inner Bitch. I honestly can't think of a bad word to say about anyone.

A: LIAR. No one – *no one* – is that nice, that perfect or that kind. We all have a nasty side. You passive-aggressive bitches who never say a bad word about anyone still have the internal dialogue, no matter how hard you try to pretend that it is not there, or try to silence it through 'niceness'. You are no better than the loud-mouthed bitches who shout and let us know when they are pissed off. We all have a nasty side, be it silent or otherwise. The sooner you make friends with this, the better off you will be.

MIRROR, MIRROR

Please remain fully clothed for the following exercise. (You RFBR nutters know what I'm talking about . . .) Stand in front of the mirror. First, warm up your IB by closing your eyes and thinking about that vexing person/situation until your blood starts to simmer. OK, great.

Without further ado, open your eyes and say loudly, accompanied by scowly face, BUILD THOSE EFFING SHELVES YOU USELESS LAZY BITCH!

PART 1

ACTION

1

LIGHTS, CAMERA, ACTION!

So, holding hands with your Inner Bitch, I hope you are feeling pumped about the idea of bringing an action-taking approach to all areas of your life. Always bear in mind, when this feels too much like hard work, that *it is supposed to be hard work*. Life is hard. Very hard. But hard is no longer something we are going to shirk or try to avoid at all costs. Hard is the new black. Grit isn't a tasty word – it is coarse, granular, bitty. For good reason. Roll it around on your tongue and make friends with it. Because it has to be swallowed without complaint on a daily basis in order to remain in GYSTful swing, which is always the aim.

THE GRIT DOCTOR ANNOUNCES:

Let grittification commence.

THE GRIT DOCTOR WILL SEE YOU NOW

Q: But how do I know what action to take, and how do I decide what to do first?

A: Don't waste too much time on this one. The crucial thing is

to begin. To start on something, anything, *but* make sure it is necessary and relevant to GYST. So, for example, if you want to take up life drawing, enrolling in a local art class would be an action that was both necessary and relevant to the goal in mind. Watching the last episode of *The X Factor* on catch-up is an action, and may well be on your To Do list, but it sure as shit isn't the kind of action I'm referring to. A key distinction to draw from the off is that *activity* is not to be confused with *action*. You know those busy-bee, chaotic types who are always rushing about the place, picking things up and putting them back down again? *That does not count as action*. That is a waste of time and incredibly irritating to boot. Think of action as taking on a necessary task, no matter how small or seemingly trivial, and completing it. The essence of action is in its completion. Action is when the job is done. So, using the above example, the job is done when you are staring at a butt-naked man and drawing his bits.

'Never confuse movement with action.'
Ernest Hemingway

If you are reading this and feel as though you are stuck in a state of permanent inertia, and almost paralysed with inaction, then you will be delighted with the exercise below. Begin immediately.

THE SHELF EXERCISE

Spring clean *one shelf* of *one cupboard* in your home.

If you think that you don't need to participate in this exercise because . . .

a) It's my career that needs sorting out, not my cupboard

b) My cupboards are immaculate, thank you very much

c) My cleaner's coming tomorrow

. . . think again. This exercise is *compulsory* and is as important for you as for the next person. If you are reading this book and committed to getting your shit together, it all begins with that one shelf in the cupboard. **DO IT NOW**. Even if it feels like a mere formality. And do it with gusto. Repeat this exercise (not the same shelf, you idiot) daily for grit fiends and weekly for grit dodgers until all the cupboards in your home are pristine.

No matter how all over the place we think our shit is, we can *all* take this first step towards sorting it out if it involves something as straightforward as cleaning one shelf of one cupboard. No matter what sort of state we have got ourselves into, we can all do this one simple task. Once we have cleaned one shelf and succeeded, and admired our handiwork and felt really pleased with ourselves about having done it, we can then utilise this feeling of positivity by 'piggybacking' onto it to tackle the next shelf. And then, before we know it, one shelf at a time, we will have our entire home in order.

Ruth

I am going to tackle one shelf. Now I am doing it, it all seems so obvious, but one of the reasons I have avoided the kitchen cupboards' spring clean for so long is because every time I contemplate it, every time I look at it, it feels like too much to take on. I never have a long enough stretch of time to complete it — there is always something else more pressing that needs my attention, or I just can't be bothered. On the other hand, when taken on as simply one shelf at a time I am immediately attracted to the prospect of doing it NOW. Hell yeah, I can do a shelf easily. It will only take ten minutes, tops, and actually, while I am at it, I may as well do two shelves.

And this exercise acts as double-bubble because not only is it going to result in a spring clean of our homes, but it will also act as a new metaphor in our lives. *Oooh, sounds deep.* What I mean is that we can *all* clean a shelf. As jobs go, it actually wasn't too taxing, nor did it take too much time. But The Grit Doctor also wants you to think of 'the shelf' as the metaphorical first step to take in any overwhelming project. When broken down into bite-sized chunks – shelves – that insurmountable problem/project becomes something different, something perfectly palatable. And therein lies another GYST key: developing the skill of looking at a project or task or life-changing biggie and working out how to break it down into 'shelves'.

THE GRIT DOCTOR SAYS:

'One shelf at a time' is always the way forward.

And this is how stuff gets done. It is, in fact, how *everything* gets done – even the really big things, the ideas and concepts, the life-changers. They all begin with the shelf.

GRIT-MANIA

Once you have become an action-taking aficionado, you will no longer be paralysed by the really difficult task or be tempted to put it off until later, when all the other easier ones are done. You will instead tackle the hardest, grittiest project first. Why? Because the more gristle you develop, the more you appreciate the real value in getting the most difficult thing out of the way first. It buys you time. Putting it off has a tendency to mess with the rest of your day to such an extent that you will literally be creating other stuff to do – meaningless time-wasting tasks and 'activity' – just to avoid doing it. (Remember those elaborate revision charts, created at the expense of any *actual* revision?) But if that sort of grit-mania seems a long way off, worry not. Slowly slowly, catchy monkey.

Now some of you may actually have half-decent gristle already, which has gone a bit flabby through recent neglect. Others may never have located their gristle at all in their lives, let alone flexed it. Some of us need a rocket up our arses just to winch ourselves off the settee, others want to be able to do more in less time and don't know how. Some may feel dissatisfied with their lot and don't know why. Some of you may at this stage be telling yourselves that you are happy doing nothing and The Grit Doctor can bugger off. You are deluding yourselves. If that were the case you wouldn't have read this far, nor would you have been drawn to this book in the first place. The gritty truth is that human beings all thrive on doing stuff and even more so on completing stuff. We are less ourselves when we are inactive: we languish, we shrink. But when we are busy completing tasks and achieving things, no matter what they are or how big, small or insignificant, it somehow calls forth our better natures. So don't get caught up in the bullshit argument that you are truly happy doing nothing. I don't believe you. You don't believe you. You need to WAKE UP your Inner Bitch and see what she has to say on the subject.

Say you have always talked about writing a novel, but have never quite got round to it. The table on the next page illustrates how the 'shelf' principle applies.

The Procrastinator's Approach

Cleaning shelf	Writing novel	Result
Where's that new organic cleaning spray I bought? * Spends half an hour searching *	*Oh God, what shall I write about?* Spends a month thinking about 'ideas'/choosing and then doodling in fancy notebook.	Shelf gets cleaned, but only after 90 minutes of faffing. End result is an overly complicated organisational system that falls apart within weeks. You feel exhausted and completely demotivated.
Ooh, should I look on Lakeland.com for a new shelf-organising system? * Wastes half an hour online *	*I can't possibly write anything worthwhile on this crappy machine.* Spends two weeks researching new laptops.	You haven't written a word, but you have wasted hundreds of pounds on a laptop you didn't need. Your nails look *flawless*.
What music would best accompany cleaning this shelf? * Messes about on iTunes for half an hour creating 'Ultimate Cleaning Playlist' *	*Wow, my nails look a mess typing on this slick new laptop.* Delays starting writing in favour of manicure.	

The Action-Woman's Approach

Cleaning shelf	Writing novel	Result
Sort tins into those to keep (in date) and those to throw away (out of date).	Turn on computer/find a piece of paper. Start to write about the first thing that comes to mind. Keep writing for half an hour, minimum.	Shelf is cleaned in ten minutes. It is now neat and tidy and you can see the contents clearly. You feel energised and immediately look for another task to tackle ...
Wipe down shelf with damp sponge and soap.	Realise what you've written is rubbish. Delete/rip up. Start again.	You have written every day. What you have produced might not be of Booker-winning quality – *yet* – but you've developed a routine and are feeling full of inspiration.
Put the tins you're keeping back in cupboard, in a neat line.	Repeat until you've developed an idea you're happy with and have written it up.	

THE GRIT DOCTOR WILL SEE YOU NOW

Q: But what's the point of all this shelf business? I like being messy.

A: You may like being messy. I do too. But I can still acknowledge that being messy ensures my shit remains all over the place – quite literally. The first point is: we need to be in charge of our homes, to know where things are kept, to have some semblance of order, so that we don't waste the first ten minutes of each task scouring every inch of the house for the ruler, the jumper, the keys, our glasses, the phone . . . whatever it may be. It is as much about making an inventory of one's living space as anything else. In delving into each cupboard, every nook and cranny, and turning it out and cleaning it up, we find what we have been missing. *Aha. My spare set of keys!* We can clear stuff out, throw away junk, and will, in the future, better remember where things are kept – which leads to us being more efficient at dealing with life's *gritmin*.

THE GRIT DOCTOR SAYS:

90% of life is GRITMIN.

But the most crucial point is this: THE SHELF IS A METAPHOR. An untidy home may not be a problem for you. Fine. But whatever area of your life suffers from a lack of shit togetherness, you will be able to face it far more effectively if you accept the principle that *one shelf at a time* is the answer. Because whenever we feel over-whelmed by the big stuff, we can bring to mind the shelf exercise and in so doing remind ourselves that anything is possible when we are willing to address it in bite-sized chunks. Working out what 'the shelf' is may be half the battle, but sometimes the shelf order gains clarity once you start on, say, the second or the third shelf. Even if, in retrospect, it was plainly not the obvious first thing to have tackled, it matters not if the job ultimately gets done. My sister Anna's recent move to Australia is a case in point.

To: The Grit Doctor

From: Anna

Re: GYST Down Under

I emigrated to Australia on 3 November last year. I wanted to be with the man I loved (who lives in Melbourne), I had decided law wasn't for me (for now, anyway) and I wanted to explore new opportunities in a country still full of them. I booked my flight exactly four weeks prior to that date. All seems like pretty swift acting, huh? Pretty decisive and proactive. Quite the opposite actually — the decision to move took a lifetime. I created all these fake, 'deep' problems that I told myself were so insurmountable; that there was no point even investigating the option to emigrate. All this because I couldn't be arsed with the admin.

To avoid getting my shit together, the following were just a few of those insurmountable problems I made up: parents (they will be so disappointed if they can no longer say their daughter is a lawyer); family (I'll miss my brothers and sister so much, and my nephews will forget me and I won't be their favourite person); job (I will never get a job in Australia EVER. E.V.E.R); guilt (I can't leave my family to deal with my family), worry (for the sake of it); anxiety (fashionable these days — I like to be on trend); friends (they'll forget me completely) and of course the root of all woe — money, and more specifically, the fact that I had absolutely none.

So how did I get my shit together in the end? *I just booked the flight*. This move achieved three key things: 1) If I really didn't want to move because of the above 'issues', it wouldn't have been so goddamn easy to click the 'confirm flight' button; 2) as soon as I bought the flight I felt an unbelievable sense of empowerment — I had made the first and most important step to forming a life for myself off my own bat and 3) the flight cost a lot of money that I didn't have, so I HAD to get everything organised by 1 November or it would be a royal f**k up.

Those three things gave me the kick up the ass I needed. Having booked the flight, I HAD to get my visa sorted, which took all of about fifteen minutes — all that stupidity for fifteen minutes. Once I was all set to go, the above problems completely dissipated. It was only then that I realised they were never even problems to begin with; it was just me being shockingly lazy and ultimately scared of the real things, the real pressing admin that needed to be done before I left and that could be problematic. I've now learnt an invaluable lesson though: *do the real shit first* and see how it goes before making other shit up in your head. The visa was always going to take fifteen minutes to get. Had I done the research and found that out — rather than being absolutely terrified that the results of any investigations would mean that I would be stuck in the UK for another lifeless year — I wouldn't have created all that other crap, which quite literally paralysed me. Secondly, if the real shit is hard or does in fact take longer than expected, all is not lost. Wait. Keep at it. If you stop it'll be because you're being lazy — and guaranteed you'll be making shit up to excuse it all. Don't let the fear of failure prevent you from trying in the first place.

Anna tackled the final shelf first in her quest to emigrate Down Under (buying the plane ticket before saving up adequate funds or investigating visa options) and is a brilliant example of how it doesn't matter if you get the shelf order wrong, but that obsessing about getting it right can paralyse you from taking any relevant action at all.

THE GRIT DOCTOR SAYS:

There are no prizes for getting the shelf order right. Just get the job done.

Ruth

I bought a small garden shed over the summer, via Olly. By that I mean, having decided that we needed one and figured out where it could reasonably fit in our small garden, I delegated the job of finding and choosing the shed to Olly. This he did, after a great deal of internet research. I got our handyman to come over, erect it for us and paint it (the paint came free with the shed). It took him the best part of a day and involved all sorts of 'technical' things – levelling the ground, building a base and so on – so I was hugely relieved that we had asked him to do it rather than attempting it ourselves. The only problem was the paint – it was disgusting, a really virulent shade of green. Decidedly unattractive.

33

'NOOOOOOO!' screamed The Grit Doctor. Instead of ignoring her call to arms (by switching on the telly, or pouring myself a large glass of wine) I instead marched to the shops and purchased some lovely green paint at the first opportunity I had, capitalising upon the urge before it faded into dull resignation. I took advantage of my sister who was visiting that Saturday, and together we re-painted the shed while the twins had their afternoon nap. Job done. From deciding to get a garden shed to having it up and painted (the right colour) took a fortnight.

THE GRIT DOCTOR SAYS:

The longer you leave between hearing your Inner Bitch and obeying her demands, the less likely you are to take any relevant action at all.

The first job (the shelf) was to decide where in the garden to put the shed, which I did myself. The next job involved delegating to Olly the business of measuring up the space and then choosing and ordering the shed. Yes, I was perfectly capable of doing this myself, but the truth is I would rather not – internet research is a particular weakness of mine and I am married to someone for whom it is a strength, so to me this was a no-brainer. The next step was hiring someone to build it. All delegation. I just painted it with my sister. The point is that it got done, fast, and I consider it to have been my work, but Olly, the handyman and my sister were all key components in the process.

THE GRIT DOCTOR SAYS:

DELEGATE. There is more than enough grit in our lives that *we have to suck up* without adding unnecessary extras into the mix.

The point of sharing this rather unsexy tale is to illustrate several important things about GYST. GYST never means insisting on doing everything by yourself. The art of delegation is absolutely key and will ultimately lead you to get more done in less time with a great deal less stress, leaving you with more free time to spend as you please. Stress rears its ugly head when we are confronted by a task that we feel is beyond our capabilities, or outside our remit. This (that it is beyond us) may not be true but our conviction that it is ensures anxiety and, often, paralysis. *The task will not get done.* Which is a crying shame if all we actually needed to do was outsource the job to someone else who was available and willing to help. And this doesn't invariably mean paying anyone, if you are clever about it.

So, never allow yourself to be put off doing stuff – especially DIY stuff – because of your lack of experience or fear of failure. The reason there is such a thing as a handyman is because it is a highly prized skill. Find one. Make him godfather to your first born and have him on speed-dial. Never invite him, or indeed her, round to do one thing at a time – make it much more cost effective by combining the job with others that need doing. And while the handyman is in your lair, ask him politely to do other things which he will find a cinch, but will floor you and your other half for the rest of the year (hang mirror/bathroom cabinet/fix door knob/do the loft conversion … Okay, possibly not the loft). With any luck he will do this for a nominal charge, or even for free, because you have paid him already for the proper job, plied him with cups of tea and been nice, *and* dealing with all three of those extra jobs (bar the loft conversion) would set him back all of about fifteen minutes with his power drill to hand.

THE GRIT DOCTOR SAYS:

Yes, you are taking advantage – a fundamental skill to develop in GYST. Provided you allow others to take advantage of you too, AND YOU ARE UPFRONT ABOUT IT, fair's fair. So get off your high horse and make friends with the idea.

As already mentioned, I *hate* searching the internet for products or comparing prices or analysing reviews. I am useless at it and do not have the patience. My husband, as I have already mentioned, is a master of this art. Great. Wherever I can, I delegate it to him. It's a *quid pro quo* situation – there's plenty of stuff I have to do in lieu. When it comes to subjects as riveting as sheds, or car insurance, if you don't have an other half who is good at or willing to take on this area for the both of you *and* you *abhor* it to the extent that you will avoid dealing with it at all costs, as I do, consider piggybacking onto the research of a particularly anal friend who you know goes through all this shit with a fine-tooth comb. Ask them for help. They will be chuffed to bits at having been asked and their research will dramatically cut down on the need for your own. And yes, okay, your friend may not have exactly the same criteria as you when it comes to home-contents insurance/wills/electricity suppliers, but using their research efforts by adapting their findings to suit your situation is bound to reduce the amount of time you will have to spend on it. They may even offer to do the research for you, so strong is their love of such tasks. Bingo. The deal here, of course, is that when the same friend wants help from you with something you excel at, you oblige. *Quid pro quo*, remember?

You may of course not give a damn about the comparative costs of various services, and if you can afford to be cavalier about these things, fine. But do consider that if managing money is a weakness of yours, and an area that needs GYSTing, then this sort of admin is both pertinent and necessary for you. So rather than flying in and getting the first thing you come across without consideration of the alternatives, resist the urge, get gritty with yourself and do as I suggest.

THE 'SHELF' IN ACTION

To: The Grit Doctor

From: James

Re: Digging for victory

I left university £20,000 in debt and eventually went into a media job which paid so little, my financial situation quickly deteriorated. I was always skint. It was only when I went to visit a pal nine years or so ago that things started to change for me. He was lucky enough to have a garden — albeit an incredibly overgrown and unkempt one — and I offered to help him sort it out. I had always enjoyed keeping plants in my flat and I was desperate for extra cash — this seemed like an obvious solution. Each Saturday I would go over and get digging. My mate soon offered me more money — enough money, in fact, for me to properly landscape the entire garden. I really enjoyed the experience. I was by this stage working full time in the arts world, primarily fundraising. But I saw in that one job for my friend that I could make much better money from working outside, doing a job I loved. I bought a few tools, my parents gave me a proper fork and spade and I gradually started to pick up other jobs — which I would pack into every Saturday — from clients I met through my fundraising activities. I worked six-day weeks for six years — three of those years on my own. It was knackering and I had no energy to think of expanding it any further — I simply couldn't, given the demands of my full-time job.

My breakthrough came in 2009 when a great mate of mine died suddenly and I had that sense of

how short and how unpredictable life is. So I
got cracking: I built a website, made T-shirts
and flyers, got myself some serious power tools
and took on a few proper landscaping projects.
But I was still afraid of giving up the safety
net of my 9—5. Eventually I got a four-day-a-
week maternity cover job. I was under much less
pressure and had bags more energy from the
extra day's rest. When the maternity cover came
to an end, I took the plunge and set up the
business full time, having consulted numerous
friends for advice. Everybody said to do it —
without kids or a mortgage, I suppose I was in
a good position to take a risk and so I did
just that. I would be lying if I said I didn't
have a few sleepless nights — I did — but it
was amazing how the business just snowballed.
Before I'd even had the chance to tell people,
I was getting calls and bookings for work — it
was as if just in the act of finally making up
my mind and committing to doing it that work
got generated. I now have six people working
for me and we have only been going for two
months! At the moment I am working seven days a

week and am always on call, putting in fifteen
hours a day. But I never have time to watch the
clock. And I know working these crazy hours
won't be for ever. The days just fly by and I am
so excited to be in charge of my life — it
feels as though for the first time.

James tackled a biggie — career. Looking back on his story you can see how it breaks down nicely into 'shelves' every step of the way, and that it all involved taking action — action that was both necessary and pertinent to the end goal. I'm sure he spent many nights lying awake dreaming of his successful gardening business, but what created it, what brought it about, was simple commitment and hard graft, going that extra mile, putting in six-day weeks, gritting it out, looking for opportunities and exploiting them, and *just getting on with it.* It took nearly ten years to make it a reality and I'm afraid therein lies another gritty truth. Dreams don't become reality overnight, but taking action towards rooting them in reality transforms them from the dream state into a work in progress, which shifts the dynamic immeasurably. It will finally *be happening.* It will have begun, and that in itself will generate an enormous amount of energy to further progress your project.

JAMES' SHELVES

- 'I offered to help him sort it out'

- 'Each Saturday I would go over and get digging'

- 'I bought a few tools'

- 'I built a website, made T-shirts and flyers, got myself some serious power tools and took on a few proper landscaping projects'

- 'I consulted numerous friends for advice'

- 'I took the plunge and set up the business full time'

'Have a bias towards action – let's see something happen now. You can break that big plan into small steps and take the first step right away.' *Indira Gandhi*

If career or job is your biggie, the first thing you need to do is to identify what is necessary and relevant in your quest (look for the 'shelf') and then start taking the appropriate action.

The temptation here is to dive into a frenzy of list making: of the pros and cons of your current job or your strengths and weaknesses as an employer/employee, or your thoughts and aspirations, where you want to be in five years' time – all of which will get you nowhere. It may well lead to you feeling even more confused as your hopes and dreams once again become consigned to crumpled pieces of paper discarded into (or just outside of) the waste paper basket.

THE GRIT DOCTOR SAYS:

STOP WRITING LISTS. Just sit down, take a deep breath and start ordering your thoughts *in your head.* When they have achieved some semblance of clarity and flow, then is the time to pick up the pen. But not to write a list. Put down the pen again, please. Focus. Breathe. Read on.

 THE GYST FACILITATOR

The table is an invention of utter genius. Not the one where you eat dinner, but the sort already seen on page 27. In the course of writing this book, table-making became a key tool in organising and ordering my jumbled thoughts on a great deal of the subjects. I have come to love the table with such a passion that I have elevated its status to that of **The GYST Facilitator**. No, it is not a list. A list is just random things to do in no particular order, requiring only the bare minimum of thought. A table of the kind I have in mind is a different animal altogether. It requires that each item on it has a specific purpose and leads on to a specific next step. It necessitates being organised, and requires some ordered thinking. So much shit gets done in the thinking stage (beware internal waffle, and do listen out for your Inner Bitch to help sift the wheat from the chaff). So, careful consideration is always essential before anything gets written down. It matters not whether this is done with pen and paper or on a computer. Use whichever medium you work most effectively and efficiently with. Start ordering your thoughts into rows and columns.

THE GRIT DOCTOR SAYS:

If in doubt, or when confused, clean a shelf and order your thinking while you are at it.

On the next page you can see the sort of thing The Grit Doctor has in mind, with a few pertinent examples.

THE GYST FACILITATOR

SHIT-TOGETHERNESS GOAL	HOW TO ACHIEVE AND TIMEFRAME	WHAT'S STOPPING YOU?	WHAT 'SHELVES' ARE NECESSARY TO ACHIEVE GOAL?
Sort out career.	Get new job. *By 1 October – at which point I'll have been in current job for five years.*	*I'm so unhappy at work I have no energy to change the situation. Finding a new job is so time consuming and I probably won't get anything I apply for anyway.*	1. Find old CV and update ⇩ 2. If there are gaps in CV, look into training ⇩ 3. Look for opportunities in newspaper job pages/online ⇩ 4. Send to recruitment agencies ⇩ 5. Schmooze contacts
Make spare room into functional space.	Declutter and buy sofa bed. *By time friend visits in two weeks.*	*Agh, there's too much stuff. Every time I open the door I feel overwhelmed and just close it again. I can't even see where the bed would fit!*	1. Get one black bin bag, attack room until filled with stuff for charity shop ⇩ 2. Continue to sort clutter into stuff for charity shop/stuff to throw out ⇩ 3. Take stuff to charity shop ⇩ 4. Measure space for sofa bed, go online and order
Host dinner party for husband's birthday.	Cook dinner for eight without dying of stress and murdering guests. *Birthday is in five days' time.*	*What will I make? What if it turns out wrong? What if no one talks over dinner? I'm a rubbish cook, I hate entertaining and I have nothing to wear.*	1. Decide on recipe – an old favourite – ard cook in advance* ⇩ 2. Order ingredients online, or buy in shops, a few days before dinner party and decide on outfit ⇩ 3. Set table, pour glass of wine – relax!
Sort out disastrous love life.	Go on a minimum of two dates. *Within next two months.*	*I can never meet men. I hate going on dates – they're so awkward. I'd rather stay at home with a good book.*	1. Swallow pride and sign up to a dating website – and commit to responding to at least one message in every five ⇩ 2. Ask trusted friend to set you up with any eligible bachelors she knows ⇩ 3. Treat yourself to new 'date outfit' – a sort of sexy uniform in which you will be interviewing prospective candidates for the role of love of your life

*On the subject of dinner parties, The GD advises stew/curry/coq au vin – something that actually tastes even better for having been cooked the day before. Nothing more stressful than actually cooking when the guests arrive. And, if you *really* don't have anything to wear – I bet you do – then when you're ordering your groceries online, you can also buy yourself something to wear. Maybe not from Tesco.

Use a table like this – adapted to suit you – to order your thoughts when you're facing a task or problem which feels overwhelming. Remember, the important thing is to identify the first shelf, the easily achievable task which will set the ball in motion. The rest should flow from this one simple step. Setting a timeframe for your goal is compulsory. It is amazing how demotivating it is to set yourself a goal of 'somewhere, someday I will . . . ' It has a habit of disappearing off into the atmosphere and remaining forever out of your reach. Time-binding your efforts, on the other hand, keeps the show on the road, with the shelves clearly visible, enabling you to nail them one by one as you move closer towards the end goal.

With that in mind, this is one of those occasions where The Grit Doctor expects you to show some initiative and design a table which best suits the way your mind works and which will help you get the job done. Use the template on the opposite page as a jumping-off point if it helps you. It is not about designing the perfect template – it is about ordering your thoughts and creating some clarity and flow to your action-taking thereafter.

It bears repeating here that the key to getting better at **Being In Action** is to try to simplify stuff, to break it down into actions that you can take rather than creating more obstacles or complications which prevent you from actually doing anything to realise your goal. The steps, once identified, may be very straightforward, but of course behind the 'shelf' lie a million different possibilities and options. But none of this changes what must happen to begin

THE GYST FACILITATOR

SHIT-TOGETHERNESS GOAL	HOW TO ACHIEVE AND TIMEFRAME	WHAT'S STOPPING YOU?	WHAT 'SHELVES' ARE NECESSARY TC ACHIEVE GOAL?
			1. ⇨
			1. ⇨
			1. ⇨

the process. Nothing is going to happen while you are thinking about what to do. Obvious, yes, but we can spend an entire lifetime in the pre-shelf phase. It is only when we take the action, the first necessary step, that the dream becomes a work in progress. Paradoxically, it is the action itself that often brings forth the idea, the opinion, the THING. Think of actions as possessing magical qualities or fairy dust. **Action always generates good stuff, and loads more of it than you can possibly imagine.**

A great friend of Olly's – who shall remain nameless – is a phenomenally successful businessman and a case in point. He worked as a computer programming contractor for a leading newspaper's travel price comparison website, and after seven months, was approached by his boss and a sales guy about setting up on their own.

```
To: The Grit Doctor


From: Anonymous


Re: The school of hard knocks


The business at the paper was profitable, but
the expenses were ridiculous and we thought we
could do it better. So we waited for my
```

contract to end and played around with some business ideas. I saved up and took out a loan and we launched within three months — effectively using the template from the newspaper's price comparison site but adapting it and creating what we thought was a better model. I worked from home to begin with and talked via Skype, keeping costs to a minimum. Internet businesses are really good in this way as they don't necessarily involve big start-up costs. It was 2005. We sold the company in 2011, by which time it was turning over £7 million — and it wasn't the best in the business by any means, it was the fourth or fifth biggest website of its kind. We made so many mistakes — I call it my MBA, as it cost about the same in terms of the money I lost through all the things I got wrong in that first year. But failing and cocking things up was absolutely key to our eventual success — it was the school of hard knocks.

No grand new idea, and nothing original. Just three ambitious guys who saw an opportunity to do something better than the way it was being done, and crucially, rather than just talking about it on a Friday night over a beer, they translated their vision into an actionable business plan and got cracking. Now, if they wanted to, they could all now retire on the proceeds . . .

THE SHELVES:

- We identified an opportunity to create a better website

- We played around with business ideas

- I saved money

- I took out a loan

- *Worked insanely hard (I've added this in as I know the hours and commitment and dedication he put into it)*

- We launched new website three months later

- **I made mistakes** to the tune of the cost of an MBA

Ruth

My mum pointed out to me recently how the twins are beginning to grasp the basic principle of cause and effect: when I press this button, the clown pops up. When you take a specific action, a specific result will occur. It is sobering to realise that somehow, during the course of their lives, this vital skill will get obscured, and possibly lost. When the link between cause and effect becomes blurred, we can find ourselves spending too much time doing really pointless tasks: looking busy but not getting shit done, if you get my drift. Good news: Gristle will help you resurrect it. You do something – X – because you expect or know from experience that something else – Y – will happen. Going about tasks willy-nilly, without an expectation of Y happening, will have you behaving like a hamster in a wheel, frantically busy and running out of energy fast but achieving next to nothing. You have to work out what the point is first. Time spent thinking – which means actually structured thinking and not daydreaming – is vital. Doing less to get more done is the aim. And it is only done when it is done, when it is finished. Stop starting loads of things and finishing none of them. It is irritating for everybody, but most of all for yourself. Your Inner Bitch hates this approach. Keep her satisfied by feeding her completed tasks, done and dusted. Always ask yourself, Why am I doing this? Is it essential or relevant or is it just faff in disguise, displacement activity or procrastination?

LET LOFTY STAY LOFTY

It is great to have lofty ambitions, to aim high, to dream about glory and success, an amazing home, a better body, a more satisfying career, a more fulfilling marriage. And all these things are within reach, all are possible, but *only* when we break them down and tackle them one shelf at a time. Having the ultimate goal, holding the dream in our minds and cherishing it is important if it motivates us to tackle the shelf, but not if it remains firmly stuck in fantasy mode and prevents us from taking those small and necessary steps every day that are consistent with its becoming a reality.

Lofty ambitions and daydreaming are becoming problematic if any one of the following sounds familiar to you:

- You have spent so much time daydreaming, while eating chocolate on the sofa, that you actually have a name for the pet dog that you and your fantasy husband own and have chosen the soft furnishings for the 'library' and every other room in your chateau in France.

- Your fantasy life bears no relation whatsoever to who you are, and where you are, and no amount of grit doctoring could make it a reality (becoming an astronaut who discovers a new source of energy, and saves the world while cohabiting with an alien on Neptune for example).

- What you dream about would actually be harmful to yourself and others were it ever to become a reality.

- Your lofty ambition has only ever occupied head space, has never been voiced or shared and stops you doing anything useful because you believe that somehow this crazy fantasy life is miraculously going to happen to you while you close your eyes sucking a toffee. For example, you start daydreaming about your fantasy career as a tennis pro while watching Wimbledon, and by the time you are jogged back into reality, the entire day has passed and the only useful activity you have participated in meanwhile are your own ablutions.

THE GRIT DOCTOR SAYS:

GET A GRIP. If you are a thirty-two-year-old accountant with a gammy knee, you are never going to dance on stage with the Royal Ballet. Let the daydream go. Focus instead on something within your reach.

BASIC INSTINCT

GYST begins with mastering the basics of life through action. What are the basics?

- Home – do you have a roof over your head? Are your bills paid? Do you feel at peace(ish) when you walk through the door?

- Job – do you earn enough money? Are you doing your job well? Does it suit you?

- Relationships – are your relationships with your friends and family functional?

Focus on distilling life down to its basics, and get those right – then anything else on top is a bonus.

2

HELP YOURSELF

Ruth

When it came to writing another book after 'Run Fat B!tch Run', I was terrified. Of course, I was incredibly flattered by the notion that anyone would want to read another book by me, but once that wore off, I was left feeling completely overwhelmed at the prospect of having to actually write it. I felt like I was drowning. Who am I to write about this stuff, when clearly I don't have my own shit together? I can't write another book, let alone one as difficult as this. What does getting your shit together mean anyway? What is life? WHO AM I??????? ARRRRRGIIIHHHH. You get my drift. Every time I contemplated the whole book, and tried to grapple with the meaning of it, I got stage fright, panicked and couldn't cope with even beginning to tackle the project.

It was only when I shared my fears with a friend in the playground (we were with our toddlers, you understand) that I had one of those Eureka! moments. She suggested I start with an easy bit, rather than looking at the whole thing and feeling overwhelmed by it. Of course, begin with what you know; start with the easy, bite-sized bit. I had been oblivious to this very

obvious solution because I was so caught up in feeling
overwhelmed that I was unable to see my way forward.

BLIND SPOTS

Sometimes we develop blind spots about the problem that is worrying us the most, the really big one that is keeping us awake at night. This is particularly true when we keep the problem locked up inside our brains and fail to share it with anyone else. I wasted inordinate amounts of time and energy thinking and worrying and then thinking and worrying some more, hoping to arrive at an answer to a question I had not even yet formulated! This was both arrogant and stupid as I was failing to make use of one of the most vital resources available to all of us in our pursuit of GYST: other people. Just as delegating tasks to others dramatically reduces stress and increases efficiency and productivity, so does picking their brains and asking for their opinion.

VIRTUOUS SHIT-SORTING CIRCLES

Much like the babysitting circles of yore, a Virtuous Shit-Sorting Circle is a group comprised of a number of people whose opinion and judgement you value and respect. And to whom you would entrust the lives of your children. There can be any number within your circle, but do not let anyone in unless you are absolutely sure of their integrity and trust them implicitly. Quality not quantity is the key here. Imagine you are a contestant on *Who Wants to Be a Millionaire?* and you have your phone-a-friend option. One person on your list is brilliant at music, another at politics – you get my drift. So serious consideration is to be given to each member and what they will be bringing to the table. They don't necessarily have to be your best friends either – close friends, with the greatest will in the world, can also have vested interests.

So when you are next lying awake at night, worrying about a 'biggie', the 'shelf' might just be to pick up your phone and call one of your VSSC members to arrange a meeting. It is always best to consult your VSSC members face to face, as you will get so much more out of the conversation and the VSSC member will feel the gravitas of what is being asked of them all the more keenly, thus assuring their most considered response. Explain the dilemma clearly and, crucially, *honestly* to them and let them grapple with it. And tell them that you are looking for an honest answer. This is amazingly effective for two reasons. First, they won't have any blind spots because it is not their problem and so they are far enough removed to see the problem objectively, and devoid of emotion. This invariably leads to much better practical advice, problem solving and, ultimately, solutions. Second, they get to help you, and people love to help.

THE GRIT DOCTOR REITERATES:

PEOPLE LOVE TO HELP.

Ruth

I have often been reminded recently just how much people love to help. I was brought up to be fiercely independent and I felt that I should be able to handle everything on my own. It wasn't until I was married, really, that I realised how limiting this was. My husband (post twins, when it was painfully obvious to him that I needed help) was always saying, 'ask so and so for help', 'ask my mum', 'ask your mum'. But wow, how difficult it felt to change the habit of a lifetime. It went completely against the grain and felt totally unnatural. However, all it actually took, rather than just talking myself out of it, was to pick up the phone and say, 'I can't cope', or 'Help me, please, I think I am going mad'. I used to call my great friend Vey (number one in my VSSC for all baby-related issues) every other day and whinge and moan and weep about all the things you do when you've just had a baby and are existing on three hours' sleep a night.

Oh, and another thing. When times are tough, *any* help is worth having, even when it is far from perfect. By that I mean, even if you don't much like your mother-in-law, if she is offering to bring around casseroles and do your ironing, for God's sake let her. You just need to learn to say yes gracefully and then let her do it. This is about letting go of control, taking the help that is offered and being thankful for it.

THE GRIT DOCTOR SAYS:

Ask for help and accept the help that's offered, *even if it's not precisely the help you requested.*

Back to how much people love to help. The evidence? Think back to the last person you helped – a blind man across a road, a woman struggling with a buggy on a train, a colleague stuck on a point of law, a friend just split up from her philandering boyf. It felt good, didn't it? You probably felt special, wanted, important, possibly even an expert in your chosen field. You felt loved *and* loving all at the same time. Well, guess what? *Everyone* feels like this when they help. It homes in on a basic human instinct, calls forth our better selves and generates good feeling all round. In asking and allowing others to help, friendships are strengthened, trust grows and you give the person you have allowed to help you the freedom to ask the same of you, which you in turn will enjoy for all the same reasons. And yes, The Grit Doctor does have a cheesy side.

The same principle applies at the office, and can be used to devastating effect to help you get ahead. Ask someone really senior and influential for help. Incredibly flattering and ego-massaging for the recipient *and* it gets you noticed, builds up the relationship or helps create a relationship where none existed before. If you are trying to get ahead at work and climb the greasy pole, asking for help is a brilliant double-bubble exercise: you get the help you need, but it also puts you in direct communication with someone of influence in the company – someone you have just made feel good about themselves. And the weird thing is that once you have asked someone a small favour, they are more likely to do another one for you in the future – this is called the Ben Franklin effect. So it's official: *triple-*bubble no less, and the beginning of a beautiful relationship and quite possibly laying down the foundations for a promotion!

THE GRIT DOCTOR WARNS:

- DO NOT ask the sort of question or for the sort of favour which requires the person you're asking to DO TOO MUCH.
- DO NOT ask a question that they are not going to be able to answer without going back to university.
- DO NOT ask a question which shines a light so brightly on the depth and breadth of your ignorance

that the only option left available to the person you ask will be to make you redundant. If your knowledge gap or question is one so basic you know you would be in all sorts of shit if you owned up to it, keep schtum and Google it (or ask a VSSC member).

FACE TIME

So, the key to asking for help, and getting it, is biting the bullet and talking with someone face to face. Real human interaction – not email, not Facebook – is the *only* space in which this shit gets properly sorted out. Of course, the internet is useful to a certain degree – it is great for verification of stuff, facts, ideas and for extreme ignoramuses, as already mentioned, but it can never replace thrashing out a problem in person, because it is in the very act of engaging in a debate with another human being that things get worked out and the magic happens. Why? Because conversations develop along unforeseen lines. Because face to face, the other person can argue back, can spot weaknesses in your argument or line of thinking, can take the conversation off piste, down other unexplored avenues that your single-mindedness blinded you to. And, setting out your argument or request in an email will take so much longer than picking up the phone and talking it through. Face-to-face or voice-to-voice communication buys you time.

THE GRIT DOCTOR SAYS:

Stop being so lame and hiding behind email all the
time. Start dealing with real people IN THE FLESH.

What next? Once you have digested your VSSCs' opinion and advice
(do not waste too much time at this stage over-cogitating, please),
what is the first thing you must do? Without further ado, identify the
next shelf and take the necessary step, the action that is consistent with
the outcome you desire or the solution to the problem at hand.

A GRIT DOCTOR CAVEAT:*

Use your own judgement to assess the value of the
advice you have been given. Do not get caught up, or
worse still caught out, by rubbish advice. This caveat
is unlikely to arise if you have followed the advice on
choosing your VSSC members carefully enough. But
always rely on your own sound judgement to assess
the evidence before you. Only a total loser follows the
advice of others blindly. And yes, VSSC members can
be fired for giving shit advice.

---

*A caveat is an exception, a lovely legal term that I am very pleased to have found an
excuse to use. It is a firm favourite of The Grit Doctor's mate, The *Shit* Lawyer . . .

 THE *SHIT* LAWYER

CROSS-EXAMINING BAD ADVICE

As a criminal barrister I was often in the business of testing the reliability of a witness, trying to find flaws in their evidence by comparing and contrasting it with other evidence in the case. How do you test the reliability of the advice you have been given by your VSSC member? Pretend you are a barrister and verify it against other supporting evidence. If it is contrary to some of the other evidence available to you, then it is less than 100 per cent reliable. If contrary to *all* other evidence, then you must treat it with the utmost caution. Does it fly in the face of common sense? What does your husband/flatmate/bezzie mate have to say about it? Does it feel right? What is your gut telling you? What does your IB have to say about it? (That's your Inner Bitch, in case you had forgotten. Not your Irritable Bowel.)

In other words test it before you adopt it. Does this witness have a history of reliability and trustworthiness or are they of bad character with a history of dodgy decision making – in which case how on earth did they make it into your VSSC in the first place? Are they consistent? How does their life look to you – are they a model of GYST or the polar opposite? If in doubt, go back to square one and utilise the expertise of another VSSC member. Indeed, big decisions benefit from numerous opinions, so if it is a massive decision you are trying to work your head around (change in career/emigrating to Australia) I would seek the advice of as many VSSC members as you can get hold of before making up your mind.

THE GRIT DOCTOR SAYS:

VSSC. Sounds like the membership of an incredibly important organisation. And it is.

If a character witness in a criminal trial were the defendant's mother, how reliable do you think her testimony would be? Almost worthless, because of her relationship to the defendant. Advice is always dodgy when there is a vested interest at stake, which is why I don't recommend having family members in your VSSC. Neutral people are the answer: for work stuff, someone in a different company or with a totally different job but whose approach, attitude, discipline and judgement you admire, not your colleague who shares your desk in the office. For matters of the heart, not anyone you have any 'history' with . . .

Ruth

I got myself into a real state over the summer about my childcare arrangements. Our wonderful childminder was due to take her holiday in the first two weeks of August, so I was desperate to finish various writing assignments prior to her going away, in the knowledge that I wouldn't get a chance to do any work until her return. The week before her departure, however, one of the twins was unwell and was sent home, so I lost several more days. Three weeks of paid-for childcare, but my sick child was at home and I couldn't work. I was in a rage; I was feeling tired, frustrated and emotional and I thought, I have to change this arrangement immediately. I must get someone who comes to me instead, who doesn't mind if the babies are sick. I was so pissed off and at the mercy of my immediate 'feelings' that I had clean forgotten any of the reasons why I had chosen this arrangement in the first place. This is absurd, I am paying for her summer holiday, for bank holidays, for the days when my children are sick and can't attend and I have to get them dressed and ready and get them to her and pick them up again at the end of the day. Am I mad? Who else would put up with such an arrangement?

When I spoke to my great friend Kate (VSSC founding member) and told her my dilemma, she calmly pointed out the following and in so doing promptly provided the solution and much-needed peace of mind.

1. Didn't I need the children out of our tiny house in order to write?

2. Wasn't it, in fact, incredibly reasonably priced, even accounting for those holidays and sick days?

3. Didn't the childminder have a big house and huge garden for the twins to run around in, which I was unable to provide?

4. Didn't she also provide two nutritious, home-cooked meals for the boys?

5. Wasn't she just a ten-minute walk away up the road?

6. Hadn't I been so excited when I found her, because I 'clicked' with her right from the start and felt I could trust her implicitly with the twins?

7. And most importantly, didn't the boys love her dearly?

Kate tactfully pointed out that even twelve sick days a year was worth it. That I should write off twelve days, accept that I might lose twelve days and have a contingency plan for those days and then focus on all the reasons I had chosen this arrangement in the first place. I did just that. She is incredible with the twins, we all adore her and I once again feel very blessed to have her in our lives. And it all came about from a shift in my attitude that a good long talk with a VSSC member helped bring about.

GRIT GRENADES

Give up TO DO LISTS. Just do the most urgent thing first. Suck it up, wade into it with gusto and don't stop until it is finished properly. If you must write things down, you know the answer: The GYST Facilitator.

Get anal with your gritmin. Keep it in order so it never gets on top of you. Grit it out, at least once a week for grit dodgers and daily for grit fiends. This means filing, organising, dealing with and binning shit. The same goes for your emails and files on the computer. Don't allow your computer to become another place for hoarding junk and dumping shit. Organise and file emails and documents and use the delete function often.

Set artificial deadlines. I find this is my most useful Grit Grenade at the moment. I have been setting myself word-count targets each week and elevating them to 'deadline status' as the week progresses, to ensure that I meet them.

Always keep your CV up to date. I keep a running document alongside my CV which acts as a chronology of my life. So whenever I do anything remotely related to, or that could be construed as work, even in the loosest sense, I add it onto this document because otherwise I will forget. Having both ensures that when the time comes and an interesting job appears, you are ready to strike immediately with an up-to-date CV and a document from which you can source anything relevant to that particular job application. Even an action man can be put off applying for a job if, as well as a lengthy application form, he has the added hurdle of having to build a CV from scratch and OH NO, the deadline for applications is tomorrow. Don't let that be you.

Grittify your working environment. I've found a café near my house which is bracingly cold and without WiFi. Not so cold that I need gloves and can see my breath, but cold enough to sharpen my mind, get my legs jittery and force me to GET ON WITH IT.

Do everything you can to rid yourself of distractions. Only you know what your weak points are (refer to your list on the fridge), so figure out how to outsmart them. If you are hopeless with the internet, for example, get those apps which prevent you from accessing Facebook or Twitter while you're working. Disable hand-held devices if this is a weakness. Simplify and grittify your work space, then take a deep breath and just DO until the job is DONE.

Create a 'Grit Hour' each day in which you deal with all your most loathsome tasks. Tip: the earlier the grit hour, the more productive you will be.

Don't tie yourself down. In other words, get out of the bad habit of only being able to do certain things if a certain set of ideal circumstances exist. This can be particularly limiting for creative pursuits outside your normal 'work'. BE FLEXIBLE. Having a very set idea of where you have to be in order to do something is, frankly, crippling. When you have three kids under five, believing that you need to live in Athens for six months in order to learn Greek ensures it will never happen. Utilising a two-hour daily commute to bone up on the basics, however, creates an opportunity.

Never think 'I am too tired' to do anything. Actions generate energy. The more you do, the more you are able to do. Tiredness is a self-fulfilling prophecy. OK, so you are always tired. I know I am. Tiredness is not going to kill us. And it is far better to be tired having got some shit done than to be tired and worrying about not having done it. Never let tiredness stop you doing anything. There is always some shit that can be done, even if you are walking around half asleep. Use really tired moments, when you are completely brain dead, to do the sorts of mundane tasks that actually benefit from being zombie-esque – like sorting out the laundry.

Industrialise your cooking. This has paid huge dividends for me. Make massive quantities of the stuff you were always going to cook anyway and freeze it in batches. This saves enormous amounts of time and reduces some of the stress associated with feeding babies and toddlers. And husbands.

Make shit up. To relieve boredom over the task at hand, make it harder for yourself. Competitive swimmers keep boredom at bay by imagining sharks in the pool water. I often imagine, when bored on long runs, that I am being chased by rabid dogs. Or I set off for long runs knowing that when I return I will only have minutes to spare to collect the twins, thus ensuring I go as fast as I can. Making the margins so small means I have to be über efficient when I get back to shower, change and pick them up on time. I also only leave myself fifteen minutes to tidy the house at the end of a working day, otherwise I could waste the first four hours on housework which on writing days I consider to be a displacement activity. I enjoy this sort of frenetic activity. SWEAT THE SMALL STUFF, literally. In other words, do boring tasks really quickly so that you break into a sweat and use the least amount of time necessary to complete them. If a task isn't urgent, MAKE IT URGENT. Weaving games and shenanigans into tasks can work wonders, providing you don't get caught up in wasting time inventing overly complicated rules.

Remember that *nobody knows what they are doing*. My dad gave me this brilliant piece of advice when I was a trainee barrister. It may not be true, but it is a great way of looking at other people, rather than being intimidated and thinking they know everything. Everyone is faking it to a certain extent.

Simplify your life by dumping some shit. How to choose whether an item is dumpable? Trust your gut, and use your common sense. Ask yourself, when did I last use/look at/wear this? If the answer is: not in the last year, dump it without a trace of regret.

THE GRIT DOCTOR SAYS:

I like to call this the art of Feng Shuit.

3

FENG SHUIT

GYST begins at home. Where you live is where you are most yourself; it is where you begin and end each day. Unless and until the place you live is in order, it is difficult to adopt a productive and efficient approach to the rest of your life because you are always thrown back into chaos when you come home. The energy required to be one thing outside your home (efficient and effective) and a completely different thing at home (chaotic) leaves you feeling utterly spent. *You* begin at home, which is why cultivating a new habit of domestic order helps create the action-taking attitude to apply to the rest of your life and makes achieving it infinitely more realistic. Not only that, it lifts the spirit and primes the gristle for battle each day. Closing your front door on your way to work, leaving behind a made bed, dishes washed and a well-stocked fridge and freezer, and better still unlocking the front door when you return to a home that is ordered, does wonders for the soul.

This doesn't mean taking minimalism and neatness to such extremes that you must devote endless time and energy to maintaining it. I stress *ordered* as opposed to *tidy* because when the spring clean has been done once, and a mental inventory of sorts taken, how you choose to interpret 'tidy' is your own business. Providing it is all clean and 'shelved' and you know where the stapler is kept, how it 'looks' is a matter for you. The Grit Doctor couldn't give a shit whether your house is Scandinavian cool, vintage chic or a Magnolia + MFI masterpiece. As long as it's under control and you feel relaxed when you walk in the door, then go with whatever floats your boat. You will know when it becomes a shambles again because your Inner Bitch will have a meltdown about it on a daily basis.

Feng Shuit, once achieved on the home front, will generate a tidal wave of endorphins and action-taking, much like running. Really? I shit you not.

Ruth

My home was all over the place when I started writing this book and I realised that in order to G my ST, I had to tackle my life from the grass roots up, statrting with the tangible obvious stuff, the 'shelves', the washing, the wardrobes and all the crap I was hoarding. Why did I decide this? Because I had no idea where else to begin. And having done it – just the once – it has been relatively easy to maintain. Shelf after shelf after shelf got nailed. The GD was in my face every step of the way, channelling my gritty side, yes, but most surprisingly, liberating my mind and my mood in the process.

Getting rid of stuff from my wardrobe had an impact upon me that I could never have anticipated or imagined, even in my wildest dreams. When I finally bagged up and gave away all those clothes that I used to wear before I had the twins, I felt every bit as cleansed as if I'd had a full body detox (something I can only refer to in the abstract). I had been clinging on to them like some vestige of a past life to which I could never return. Keeping and seeing the clothes all the time made me full of nostalgia for my old life, and was preventing me from accepting where my life is now. Those short dresses and skirts and heels were holding me back from being myself and I can honestly say that bagging it all up and taking it to a charity shop gave me the same sort of freeing, peaceful endorphin rush as running a marathon or going on holiday. Because just opening my wardrobe every day was depressing me no end. Catching a glimpse of those gold glittery hot-pants that I was never going to wear again because I would look ridiculous in them. Tops that I wore to parties in my twenties that would never look right draped against the upper arm of a mother of twins. Why was I keeping them? For what purpose? To what end? They were taking up valuable wardrobe and cupboard space that I could ill afford to spare and were making me feel miserable. And look, I don't mean just because I am a mum that I am going to start dressing like a granny – I may buy myself a pair of leather trousers, who knows? – but the key difference is that they will fit me *properly and I will look good in them. Because they will be current and reflect me now.*

And no, my full-wardrobe detox was not procrastination, nor was it a displacement activity. Think back to the very first exercise: the shelf. I was tackling 'the shelf' and I was not finished until the whole house was done, which included my wardrobe. And I was writing alongside 'shelving', not shelving exclusively all day long – which is surely the road to madness. So cut me some slack, please.

THE GRIT DOCTOR SAYS:

At the heart of Feng Shui† lies a clean home free of junk and emotional baggage.

IF IN DOUBT, BURN

Junk is defined, by The Grit Doctor, as useless and/or unattractive items which clutter up surfaces while serving no function or purpose save to uglify the environment.

Be ruthless when it comes to clearing – it is both emotionally cathartic and practical. New cohabitees have a brilliant opportunity to tackle this head on, because the difficult task of melding your separate homes into a single space necessitates the brutal process of picking and choosing what stays and what has to go. Resist the urge to throw away all of his dreadful bachelor bits and paraphernalia. Actually, f**k that. Have a ceremonial burning session of all his stuff while he is away for a weekend. Oh yes, and do throw in your junk too.

THE GRIT DOCTOR INSTRUCTS:

IF IN DOUBT, BURN.

But this seems terribly unfair? Life, in case you were still deluding yourself to the contrary, *is incredibly unfair*. And as a woman you will probably find that, sadly, the job of cleaning up and taking care of the home will fall onto your broad shoulders. So it is only right in those circumstances that you get the bigger say on all matters domestic. And no, this is not anti-feminist. It is *just the way it is*. If it is the other way round in your house, great. Then he gets the bigger say. As instructed by Caitlin Moran in her brilliant book *How to Be a Woman*, I will happily stand on a chair and shout **I AM A FEMINIST**.

DOMESTIC HELP

If you are lucky enough to be able to afford help around the home, it may be accompanied by the uncomfortable sensation that you really ought to be doing it yourself. Not for me. I dread to think of the squalid conditions in which we would have to live were it not for the miracle my cleaner accomplishes in four hours every Monday afternoon. Is it somehow morally wrong to have a cleaner? NOOOOOO! screams The Grit Doctor. I give her holiday pay, free legal advice and all sorts of other perks, and she makes enough money to go home for two months every year over the summer.

The problem lies in our attitude to cleaners; that we have somehow come to view cleaning as a lowly, menial job and to look down on it. My cleaner is ruthlessly efficient and bossy and takes real pride in her work. I don't feel sorry for her or in any way superior to her, either. She is very good at her job and I pay her a fair wage for it. I also know that untidiness is a weakness of mine, so having a cleaner helps to keep it in check. A weakness of mine . . . and a catastrophe when it comes to my husband, so between the four of us we would literally be living under a pile of shit were it not for her weekly visits. The point is: keep your house clean and tidy or pay someone to help you, but either way, make sure it gets done. And don't waste time moralising about this sort of shit either. Provided you treat everyone with respect and love, there is no job in the world that is beneath being out-sourced. Not in my book.

THE GRIT DOCTOR WILL SEE YOU NOW

Q. It's all right for you, but I can't afford a cleaner . . .

A. Bad luck. This is where the shelf exercise comes into its own, literally. No fancy metaphors here. Tackle bite-sized tasks as and when they come up, rather than letting your shit pile up all week and then having to do a massive blitz at the weekend, to save your sanity. Even with four hours of help from a professional, the chaos caused by two small boys means that I have to keep on top of things on a daily basis – at least twice a day, in fact. Training infants from a young age to clean up after themselves is the key. Messy toddlers become even messier teenagers and end up having to buy a book like this in adulthood to get on top of their shit. Don't let that be yours. And it's no good shouting at them to clean up after themselves if your own shit is all over the place. We only ever lead effectively by setting the right example. I have found turning cleaning into a game to be incredibly effective with toddlers. Less so with husbands, unfortunately: the manner in which you remind, cajole or coax will pay dividends – vicious nagging, as I have learnt the hard way, never works. Everyone living in the household must be responsible for their own mess and be held to account when they don't deal with it.

GRITGASM: the incredible feeling of having cleaned all your shelves and taken all those clothes to charity, knowing where all your stuff is kept, and feeling on top of your game.

Expect multiples.

4

TIME, TIME, TIME

'Time is a created thing. To say
"I don't have time", is like saying, "I don't want to".'
Lao Tzu, ancient Chinese philosopher

Our concept of time, or our attitudes to time, have an enormous bearing on our ability to get our shit together. We all have the same twenty-four hours and yet it is patently obvious that some people achieve a great deal more than others in any given day. There are a great number of people for whom time is a real problem area. They view time as the enemy, as the source of their stress, because there are not enough hours in the day to do all the things that they need to get done, and as a result, nothing is ever finished. *And* they are never on time for appointments. In short, their time management is a shit show.

I wrote something about time in *Run Fat B!tch Run*. I always felt that the impact of having been running seemed to increase my productivity to such an extent that it was as if time had been multiplied by the run as opposed to it having eaten into my twenty-four-hour quota. This is probably on account of the rise in happy hormones that the running stimulates. It somehow has the effect of making me able to get a great deal more done with much less fuss. And furthermore, the quality of the work was always better. So I formed the view that running was an investment in time and should never be thought of as time out but, in fact, as time multiplied.

This concept can be extrapolated to include the domino effect from tackling 'the shelf' and embracing the principle of **Being In Action**. Once we are in action, our actions generate more actions which generate a good feeling when completed. Happy hormones are stimulated and we therefore have more energy for more action. This may be one of the reasons why really busy people operating in high-level jobs and working insane hours, still seem to be able to do a million times more than the rest of us in a day or week and are also rarely, if ever, heard to utter the words, *I don't have enough time, I can't do this.*

> 'You will never find time for anything.
> If you want time, you must make it.'
> *Charles Buxton*

Just as running and action-taking seem to multiply time, other activities can have the opposite, deleterious effect. The table opposite gives some examples. Feel free to add your own.

Time Thieves	Time Investors
Television	Aerobic exercise
Facebook/Twitter/internet faffing	VSSC
Fridge raiding	Good sleeping and eating habits
Whining	Grit Grenades (as seen on pp. 69–74)
List making	Talking less shit
Inactivity	BEING IN ACTION

Think of all the opportunities wasted by saying no to stuff on account of 'not having enough time', when the gritty truth is that there is always enough time. Whatever you choose to do, there is always enough time to do it, usually just enough.

Ruth

When I was living in France on sabbatical, and doing precious little, I found that whatever tiny tasks I gave myself to do on any given day – go and buy a baguette, go to the post office to post a letter – seemed to fill my whole day. I always seemed to have just enough time to do the things I had chosen to set myself to do that day. No more and no less. Now I am a deranged mother of twin toddlers, I have exactly the same amount of time in which I accomplish many more tasks.

Practise telling yourself that you will always have enough time, that time is on your side, and quit moaning about not having enough. That successful person you envy, and who you think got lucky, may well have been the person who *made time* to do something you wouldn't have. They may have said 'yes' to a request rather than 'no'. *Luck is really just choosing to exploit opportunities.* And opportunities do not always fall in your lap labelled 'Opportunity'. Au contraire. They often come disguised as accidents, sometimes even as disasters.

THE *SHIT* LAWYER

Senior silk (QC) in chambers approaches two junior barristers – both planning on taking the weekend off – late on a Friday and says: 'Would one of you draft grounds of appeal for me in this case? It's very urgent.' Junior Barrister A (JBA) lowers his head and mutters, 'I'm so sorry, but I can't, I have other commitments this weekend.' Junior Barrister B (JBB) thinks, F**K. I wanted to go on a bender after the rugby tomorrow, *but responds enthusiastically, 'Of course, I can have them with you by Monday.' The silk, relieved and thoroughly impressed, thanks JBB. JBB has, through his positive, enthusiastic response, created a very good and, crucially, lasting impression. JBB felt that the sacrifice was worthwhile, given that there would be plenty of other occasions to watch the rugby and have a good time.*

JBA was perfectly within his rights to refuse to help. But who is going to spring to mind when that silk suddenly needs a junior (a highly prized paid position)? Maybe nothing will happen in the immediate future, or maybe another favour will be asked of JBD before any 'luck' comes his way, but it is all being banked, none of it goes to waste, and the longer it remains in the bank, the more interest it earns. JBA, however, has given off the 'I'm a no man' vibe and so doesn't get asked to draft grounds the next time. He becomes better and better at saying NO, at never doing anything more than he has to, and his gristle weakens. BB, no longer quite so J, becomes a QC after fifteen years of practice and is much admired, having gained a reputation for always going the extra mile. BA becomes a criminal hack, unkindly but fairly referred to in chambers as 'dead wood'.

Sometimes the longer you have had to wait, and the more grit you have had to swallow along the way, the bigger the prize at the end, and the better position you are in to take advantage of it when it presents itself. Why? Because the attitude you develop through being a yes man and an action-taking aficionado gives you the gristle, the energy, the vim and the vision to see opportunities and the magic when it comes calling, in all its strange guises. A time-fearing, action-averse type, however, develops defects in his vision that blind him to the magic when it appears – so intent is he on desperately trying to stick to his limiting conservative time-mean schedule that he has closed himself off from all the wonderful possibilities in life that adopting the opposite approach would reveal to him.

OPPORTUNITY COST

In the making of any choice between two or more options, there *must be a loss*. THERE MUST BE SACRIFICE. This is the nature of choosing between things. We have to forgo one (i.e. the rugby bender) in order to have the other (i.e. the good opinion of the QC). A great deal of indecision lies in not accepting this basic economic principle. We hate the idea of 'giving up' the other option, so we waver for ages between two potential choices, often losing out on both as a result of failing to choose one in time. Loss is absolutely fundamental to life. We cannot avoid it, we cannot escape it, we cannot change it, so we may as well start embracing it.

The really amazing thing is that ultimately it doesn't really matter which option you choose, providing you choose one and then keep on choosing it over and over again. It is in the act of choosing that all the power lies. Not in what you choose but *that you chose it*. This takes a lot of heat out of decision making – not worrying unduly about having made the right choice all the time. It will always be the right choice if you make it so by choosing it to be. So, *get on with it*.

THE WAR ON TV

Two of our biggest enemies, the two weapons of mass destruction in the war against shit togetherness, are telly and hand-held devices. Your television set, or two, are your primary time thieves. Television is the arch-enemy of GYST. Whenever you hear yourself thinking (because of course you will never be heard to utter these words again), 'I don't have time', ask yourself immediately the following questions:

1. Who do I want to win *Strictly*?

2. Who is my favourite judge on *The X Factor* and which contestant would I most like to see suffering a nervous breakdown on stage?

3. Could Mr Bates, in fact, be a baddie?

If you can even understand any of the above questions, you are giving away far too much of your most precious resource – time – to a square box in the corner of your living room that will give you nothing back in return. If you are in denial at this juncture because you don't watch these programmes, then ask yourself if you still knew the answers. If you did, chances are you've been reading trashy magazines. Shame on you. Or worse still, found yourself discussing a TV show *you haven't even seen* with another human being! You what? This is some of the lowest-grade chat that exists and must be stamped out.

For those of you who are feeling completely lost reading this section of the book and haven't a clue about the answers to any of the questions above, you can give yourselves a pat on the back and skip this section. Anyone who could answer all three questions with confidence is giving away up to one full day a week to the principal time thief. And I bet you find yourself saying 'I don't have time' all the time.

The point of this rant is this: we will always find time to watch telly. No matter how busy we are, or how much we have going on, how stressed we feel, how urgent the project is or how long we have delayed it, we will still find time to watch telly and we are all in a state of permanent denial about it. Anyone who doesn't watch *any telly at all* would almost certainly have no reason to read this book because I guarantee that they have got their shit together. Just think how many 'shelves' we could get nailed during just one weekend's *X Factor/ Strictly* session. Anyone who says they don't have time to exercise, I challenge you to ask yourself whether you were planning to sit down at any stage this evening to watch television. If the answer is yes, then bingo: that is your exercise time.

It all boils down to the simple fact that there is always time to do the things we choose to do. *Always*. At the time of writing, *The X Factor* is on for about *five hours* every weekend. And yes, I have been watching it. And yes, I hate myself for it.

To redeem myself, instead of watching *The X Factor* from beginning to end on Saturday night, I:

- Wrote 1000 words for this book

- Had a bath with a facemask on, while reading a novel

- Feng-shuitted the bathroom cupboard to death

And I even managed to hear my favourite sing, which only took ten minutes out of my evening.

During *The X Factor* on Sunday, I:

- Put a load of washing on and sorted out the ironing

- Wrote thank you notes for the twins' birthday pressies

- Read yesterday's papers

And I still watched the elimination at the end. This exercise is perfect if you share your living space with an *X Factor* addict – it means you can watch the good bits and feel über smug for getting all this other stuff done while your other half/flatmate has had their evening stolen.

If I were to multiply this amount of activity by the remaining number of episodes, I might quite possibly have changed the world by Christmas. OK, maybe not, but the house will be immaculate, the freezer will be bulging at the seams with food to keep us going in the event of a nuclear holocaust and all my grit-min will be done. Or if I were a more adventurous type, I might have learned a foreign language, begun studying for a Master's or learnt to sculpt in bronze.

The important point is that the choice to watch telly is also a choice not to do something else.

It involves an opportunity lost every time: all those hours that could be spent starting on a new project, getting fit, building shelves (both literal and metaphorical), finding a new career, having sex, going to the theatre, the cinema, seeing an exhibition, talking to your granny, visiting a lonely neighbour, doing an art class . . . the list is endless. Every time we switch the TV on and sink into the sofa, we are also choosing not to do X, Y and Z. **And this is fine. But acknowledge the choice and stop complaining about not having enough time**. Choose to watch *The X Factor* and *Strictly* by all means, but don't go moaning when another year has passed you by and you have singularly failed to achieve any of your New Year's resolutions and find yourself a bit fatter, a bit worse off, a bit older and a bit more boring with chat so low-grade it has actually started to develop a faecal aroma.

 **SQUARE EYES**

An exercise you're going to hate. Suck it up.

For grit fiends: Try giving up telly for a month and take up something else instead. Actively take up a new hobby or use the time to do something you've 'never had time' for before. (Apply the 'shelf' principle to identify what to do and help galvanise you into action.) Why not start reading that complete set of Dickens you bought two years ago and haven't touched since? In doing something useful, productive and/or genuinely engaging you will feel a million times better about yourself. This is an exercise that your Inner Bitch is going to love you for participating in. She hates telly and loves an evening's life drawing with a passion so fierce you will wonder how you could have starved her of it for so long. And look, the telly isn't going anywhere, you can always go back to it next month, and as far as *The X Factor* goes you will have missed nothing except the four worst contestants getting eliminated. When I put it like that it does seem slightly insane to be watching it when at least half of the people involved bug the living shit out of me. I am taking this challenge on – save for *Homeland*, which is essential, Grit Doctor-approved viewing.

For grit dodgers: Try streamlining your viewing a little – or a lot. Think of each hour of the twenty-four available to you each day as a window of opportunity. Windows in which you have the opportunity to create something new for yourself and your life, whatever that may be. If you can't be arsed to take on something new, consider instead how much more enjoyable telly will be once those niggling jobs are done and dusted. The washing and ironing finished, the gritmin under control. I enjoy nothing more than sinking into the sofa for *Homeland* on a Sunday night once dinner is made and cleaned up, the washing done, and the house back in reasonable shape after a weekend of twin carnage. I wouldn't enjoy it nearly so much otherwise. It is the treat that awaits me when all my gritmin is complete. So with all this in mind, why not watch *The X Factor* on catch-up and fast forward all the acts you hate, all the boring extras, and all of Louis Walsh's comments (a man for whom my loathing is so disproportionately intense that I suspect the experience of watching the show is somehow eating away at the very core of my humanity).

As for box-set mania (you know, that feeling that you just have to watch one more episode before you go to bed . . . and then you realise it's actually 3 a.m.) – brilliant for mums with newborns caught up in the almost constant feeding frenzy that defines those early months. For the rest of us, an occasional treat to be enjoyed *only* when GYST is in full swing. I have *Mad Men* series five lined up for when I've finished this book.

THE GRIT DOCTOR SAYS:

Next time you are tempted to whinge or complain about a lack of time, ask yourself whether that task, and a million others like it, could have been completed had you chosen to smash the remote control with your shoe.

SOCIAL MEDIA: FRIEND OR FOE?

Twitter can be a lifeline for stay-at-home mums who do not have the time to read any newspapers, or books, or have conversations longer than twenty seconds. It really is a brilliant way of keeping your hand in, keeping abreast of what's going on and giving you a laugh when you might otherwise have thrown yourself under a bus. I discovered it when forced to get involved by my editor with promoting RFBR, and found it to be a real tonic through the long, lonely days with twin babies. It was a link to a world that I had almost forgotten existed and was quite sure had forgotten me. This was a completely unexpected side effect and entirely unrelated to its primary purpose (promoting my book), but I just loved communicating with other runners, other struggling mums, other people who in that moment of communication seemed to be right there with me, in the same boat. And the beauty of it? It is quick and its pared-down nature appeals to me enormously. It necessitates being clear and concise. Hours spent scrolling down your timeline, obsessively checking follower numbers (not that I *ever* do that) are, clearly, devilish time thieves, so all use of social media, whether it be Twitter or Facebook or whatever the latest new-fangled thing is, requires the application of ruthless grit management.

Too much time on Facebook can ensure that we never see anyone's *actual* face in the flesh, but instead remain glued to a screen looking at the faces of people so tenuously connected to us that, more often than not, have no real bearing on our actual lives. It robs us of vital face-to-face time with real friends and encourages voyeurism and envy of the worst sort. It makes us depressed. Streamlining our Facebook use is an absolute must for GYST, for me every bit as much as you.

THE GRIT DOCTOR SAYS:

Telly is the time thief, and social media its cunning accomplice.

	Twitter		Facebook	
	Positive uses	Negative uses	Positive uses	Negative uses
	Following news services, helping you keep abreast of what's going on in the world.	Following tweets about a television programme *while you are watching it*. You are not really paying attention to either – massive time suckage. The exception to this is if you're forced to sit through all five hours of Eurovision and the only way to get through it is by reading sarky tweets from @caitlinmoran.	Organising events – Facebook can be a great way to let people know about an event/party and manage the RSVPs.	Constantly uploading pictures of your baby in cute fancy-dress costumes. Your friends will start to hate you. Ditto pics of you in your wedding dress. Acceptable for one week after your wedding. Then stop.
	Following interesting people who will point you in the direction of stories, websites and other people you might not have come across otherwise, including those whose views are the polar opposite of your own: sharpens and broadens the mind.	Following numerous comedy/spoof accounts and endlessly retweeting their witticisms. See also the time-wasting black hole that is retweeting cute pictures of kittens/puppies.	Keeping a track of key events in B-list friends' lives – birthdays, weddings you're not invited to but would still like to send a card for, etc.	Obsessively stalking your ex/your ex's new girlfriend/the girl who bullied you in school whose life is now a disaster. This way madness lies. And you'll inevitably see something you wish you hadn't.
	Following people in your field of interest to make contacts, learn about latest developments and promote work you're doing.	Following your favourite celebs and trying to engage them in Twitter chat. THEY DO NOT WANT TO TALK TO YOU. You are not friends with Stephen Fry.	Building a community of fans/like-minded people around a particular topic (NOT YOUR CAT/FAVE TELLY PROG) and promoting your wares through regular postings. Good if you're trying to build a small business, for example.	Playing ridiculous games which kill your brain cells and clutter up your friends' newsfeed.
	Communicating with people in the same boat as you – stay-at-home mums, freelancers working at home, runners training for the same marathon.	Being mean/trolling *anyone* – even the most objectionable of celebs/politicians/sports stars. This is *never* acceptable. Show some class.	Sharing photos with family members/friends who are far away. This is acceptable.	Posting constant updates about your whereabouts etc. No one cares that you've 'checked in' at B&Q Croydon.

TIPS FOR INTERNET/IPHONE/
CRACKBERRY ADDICTS

- As a self-employed writer, I put my Blackberry on silent and then hide it from view behind the computer, and won't allow myself to look at it until a certain number of words have been written. If I am having a bad day and seem unable to comply with my own rules, I turn it off and lob it up into the loft so that recovering it requires getting a ladder and all sorts of complicated shit. If this seems extreme, do bear in mind that *my* Inner Bitch is The Grit Doctor and she is *brutal*.

- I go to the aforementioned chilly café, without WiFi. This literally doubles my daily word count. There are all sorts of apps that will disable your internet for a specific period of time. Get one. I fail at this just as much as the next person, but when I succeed, it is transformative in terms of my levels of productivity. We are all weak and we all need help to save us from ourselves. **Implement weakness decoys**. Source them from wherever you can and ask your Inner Bitch for help.

- Never have an email alert noise on your laptop. Have specific times to deal with emails and stick to them religiously. Never *ever* follow 'interesting links' during working hours.

- Whenever possible, talk to people rather than email them. It is faster, more charming, more rewarding and a quicker and more efficient use of time which leaves less room for confusion.

- If you are an adult and have a joystick for playing car games on the computer, you should be deeply ashamed of yourself. Give it up. NOW. As for 'epic' tennis matches on the Wii, for the love of God get a real racket and go outside.

SAY YES MORE OFTEN

I've never understood this fashionable thing of saying NO more. Namby-pamby self-help books which tell us we must learn to say no more often. And people who say, 'Oh yeah, that's sooooo me, I really do too much and just need to say no.' When the truth is that we all say no far too often. The confusion arises, I think, from saying yes to the wrong things, and too many of them, for the sake of looking good. (Anyone detect a faint familiar whiff of burning martyr?) Clear thinking, prioritising and saying YES more often is the answer. Being organised and doing what is necessary and pertinent to GYST. Saying yes to everything requested of you for the sake of looking good doesn't make you a better or kinder person, especially if you then whinge about it all the time. What you need to learn to do is to say yes to stuff that matters and then do it without complaint.

THE GRIT DOCTOR SAYS:

Saying yes in a martyr-ish way and feeling unfairly taken advantage of is fatal to GYST. Enthusiasm in saying yes is every bit as important as the act of saying yes. Enthusiasm applied to even the dullest of tasks will ensure it gets done more quickly and easily, with less resistance and complaint along the way. Do not make the mistake of thinking you need to 'feel' enthusiastic about something in order to be passionate about it. Practise enthusiasm at all times without getting all American about it.

Here's a little quiz to test your yes/no abilities. Look at the following questions and consider which you should say yes to (enthusiastically, even if you don't 'feel like it') and which you are entitled to say no to.

Would you mind terribly baking ten million cakes for the school's Christmas fayre? By tomorrow?

That was an interesting case you won at the Court of Appeal. Would you mind writing a piece about it for the chambers' website?

Will you collect Tommy from school again today while I get my hair done?

Can you prepare a presentation for tomorrow's 9 a.m. meeting?

Can you look after Sally for half an hour after work today while I go to the doctor's?

The correct answers are: No, Yes, No, Yes, Yes. How did you do? The Grit Doctor considers anything less than 100% correct answers to be an outright fail.

SOME TIPS ON NO

1. If you are unsure whether to say yes or no, don't hurry into an answer or allow anyone to bully you into one. You are always entitled to ask for time to consider your position. 'I'll need to check with my husband/other half/flatmate first' is always a good one for buying you some time in which to make up your mind.

2. When you say no, don't invent an excuse so intricate that you will need to create a table just to keep track of all the lies you have told. This generates enormous levels of anxiety, time is wasted and hair turns grey just from trying to keep up the artifice, when a simple 'no' would have sufficed.

3. Say no assertively and without unnecessary apology or excuse. Try to resist the urge to always dress it up. It is much more powerful and best understood when left bare. 'Thanks for asking, but no,' will do well in most situations.

THE GRIT DOCTOR SAYS:

Yes, it is gritty. I make no apology for it. People will always thank you in the end for being honest. A good, honest NO is always better than a mean, ill-intentioned YES, upon which you ultimately fail to deliver anyway.

PART 2

INTEGRITY

5

WHO AM I?

I don't want you to waste another second of your life analysing who you are and what you are really about. Self-analysis and end-lessly trying to decipher the meaning of life are without doubt two of the main causes of discontent in modern life *and* colossal time wasters to boot. Anyone who has spent even five minutes telling a stranger at a dinner party that they are 'in therapy' and have 'issues' around commitment because their parents got divorced should do everybody a favour and pipe down. Conversations analysing shit that happened ten, twenty, even two years ago are *unbelievably boring* and, in The Grit Doctor's opinion, the therapy itself is often a total waste of time and money. Not to mention responsible for some of the dullest chat ever to disgrace bars and dinner tables across the land. The only reason you might possibly not realise this blatantly obvious fact is because you have been too busy indulging yourself each week on some therapist's couch for an hour.

And look, of course your therapist is going to disagree with me. You are paying stupid amounts of money for her to tell you that this shit you are spewing is important and worth air-time. *It isn't.* Unless you are mentally ill, or have been referred by your GP for some form of specific therapy with a qualified professional for a finite period of time, you are wasting your time. The best medicine for you, without a shadow of a doubt, is to drink a small cup of shut the f**k up, remove your drowning body from Lake Me and deposit yourself on dry land.

You will never find out who you are sitting in the therapist's chair. You will just become a total bore with a very skewed and inflated idea of your own self-worth. Start from the premise that your feelings are only worth the air-time that they have in the moment that you feel them. Feel them and let them pass through you. We have hundreds of them in any given day. They are meaningless. Talking about them and trying to break them down and extract meaning from them all the time is not going to enhance the quality of your life, I'm afraid. What will is forgetting about them and getting busy *doing things to make life better for yourself and for everybody else*. It is your actions that matter, not your feelings.

THE GRIT DOCTOR SAYS:

Stop spuffing your money on therapy.

Spend the hour or two that you used to spend in therapy doing something that forces you to connect with other people: taking a cookery class, learning Spanish ... absolutely anything that forces you outside of your own head. Or, better still, go and work in a soup kitchen or women's shelter and experience first-hand how giving an hour of your time to serving other people has an impact on their lives and your own so profound that you will wonder why on earth you hadn't thought of doing it sooner.

THE GRIT DOCTOR SAYS:

Self-obsessing on a therapist's couch will not help you to love yourself. Giving that hour over to the service of others will.

THE COMPLICATED ART OF 'BEING YOURSELF'

THE GRIT DOCTOR WILL SEE YOU NOW

Q: What does 'being yourself' *actually* mean?

A: • Accept your bone structure and body shape. Of course you can (and should) work on things like fitness and health, but within reason. If you are five foot tall in heels, no amount of grit doctoring will turn you into Elle Macpherson.

   • Stop pretending to be someone else. If you can't stand French films; if you don't understand what the Credit Crunch actually is; if you really, really love One Direction, stop pre-tending otherwise. Own up – you'll feel better for it.

- Have the confidence to express your opinions. This leads on from the point above – once you have revealed your true self (ignorance about economics and questionable taste in music included) then it is much easier to express your opin-ions on all manner of subjects … and to challenge the opinions of those you don't agree with.

- Choose what to do with your life and get on with it.

I asked my Twitter followers what 'being who you are' meant to them. Here are some of my favourite responses. (See how useful Twitter can be? It's even writing my book, for gawd's sake.)

- Standing strong no matter what life throws at you

- Saying no to your mother

- Not having to change because of who's around you

- Not giving a shit what others think

THE GRIT DOCTOR SAYS:

I AM SPECIAL AND UNIQUE. Really? I very much doubt it.

You are much the same as the next person, but what will make you stand out from the crowd is the level at which you are willing to strive to achieve your goals, the lengths to which you are willing to go to be the best, the extra miles you are willing to run to squeeze another hour out of the day, the kindness you will offer a stranger, the help you will give a neighbour, the tower of strength you will be to your family during the bad times. In short, the overall effort you are willing to put into your life.

One of the most liberating things to realise is that we are not, in fact, special. GYST is not about celebrating our uniqueness or our 'special gifts'. It is about honouring our spectacular ordinariness, our perfect imperfectness, and acknowledging that none of it matters anyway. IT IS WHAT WE DO THAT COUNTS. Black, white, thin, fat, clever, thick, boy, girl, *whatever* – it is what we can achieve collectively through a common purpose, through helping each other out, through accountability, honesty and just bloody hard graft . . . that is where all the magic is at. If we focused less on our individuality and uniqueness and a bit more on our common good we would be a whole lot better off and a great deal less depressed about not looking like a supermodel too.

THE GRIT DOCTOR SAYS:

Do ordinary things with extraordinary dedication.

LOOKING GOOD

An over-emphasis on how we look is just as fatal to our well-being and self-esteem as obsessive self-analysis. And *my God*, are we in the throes of a 'looks pandemic' at the moment. The harsh truth, though, is that there is precious little we can do to change what we look like – save through diet and exercise. But instead of focusing on these two profoundly important variables and recognising just how much power we have to implement them in our lives, what do we do? We go for the most grit-free option available and chuck money at it: the latest beauty fad or crazy 'in' diet, injections, plastic, wasting thousands on con creams that promise to contain the newest anti-ageing ingredient. And this is all at the expense of trying to develop what is happening on the inside: if we spent a fraction of the time we waste looking in the mirror on developing a clearer understanding of what we are about through our actions and set out to improve our lives rather than our looks, my feeling is we would be much better off. And this doesn't mean getting all introspective either, because the best way to work out what we are all about is to *get busy doing stuff*.

A GRIT DOCTOR REMINDER:

NO, you definitely do not need to see a therapist to work this shit out.

GRIT DOCTOR BEAUTY TIPS

- **DRINK MORE WATER** to moisturise from within.

- **POSTURE** – hold yourself like a ballerina, minus the weird turned-out feet.

- **EXERCISE** helps with the smiling, glowing complexion, weight, fitness and health and wellbeing. Exercise will yield great results for your body and mind without costing you anything. I've heard about a great book ...

- **LOOK AFTER YOUR HAIR AND NAILS** – pay attention to body hair, too. I get a hair that can fairly be described as a spike on my chin that is hideous and requires plucking with pair of pliers – it seems to sprout from out of nowhere every few months. A really good haircut too can be transformative; keep nails clean and tidy.

• **STOP STUFFING YOUR FACE WITH CRAP** – eat less junk food.

• **DRESS TO SUIT YOUR BODY SHAPE** and don't draw attention to your flaws by banging on about them the whole time.

• **CONVERSATION** and **ATTITUDE** to life. A non-whingeing, non-blaming attitude, and being interested and curious about life, will make everybody fall in love with you.

• **A GREAT SENSE OF HUMOUR**. Laughing is devilishly attractive and takes years off your face. Both my mother and mother-in-law laugh easily and often, and it always makes me see them as teenagers.

• **SMILE** – keep up with your dental appointments and grit out the drill when necessary.

• **STOP SPUFFING MONEY ON MIRACLE CREAMS**. There is no such thing. Practise a simple cleansing and moisturising routine daily with products which work for *your* skin and *your* purse.

- **BE CAREFUL WITH MAKE-UP** – it has an inverse relationship to your age. The younger you are, the more you can get away with. Too much make-up past a certain age only draws attention to flaws. A make up lesson (of the non-bridal variety, all bridal make-up is deranged) is a good idea and free in a lot of department stores. Just go up to any of the counters and ask.

- **BE CONFIDENT** – this will multiply your physical attractiveness about a million-fold. Confidence will make an ordinary looking man or woman devastatingly attractive. Not to be mistaken for arrogance or control, which will detract from your looks by the same multiple. If you lack confidence, start faking it. Keep on pretending until it becomes second nature. Confidence *is a choice*.

A GRIT DOCTOR ASIDE:

You can achieve all of the above TODAY without breaking the bank.

The total cost of all the above is less than half the price of even a moderately expensive face cream. Crème de la Mer is probably the most expensive of them all and a firm favourite of some of the GD's least favourite celebs. It contains all the same essential ingredients as any basic face cream, plus a bit of sea kelp. I suppose celebs have to chuck their money somewhere, but the irony here is that most of the A-listers who swear by it actually have their faces injected with plastic all year round to maintain a line-free complexion and so have no need for the cream anyway. Which is more annoying: Botoxed celebrities who claim million-dollar creams are the answer, or those who vow that 'just soap and water' is the explanation for their smooth complexions? I can't decide . . .

Let us spare a compassionate thought for these celebs, though. Just imagine for a second, what would it feel like to be at one of their parties? We may envy their 'amazing lives', the 'fame' and 'glory', the 'money', the 'thin', the 'looks', but consider what you need to look like to walk into one of their parties and not feel suicidal. Aside from squeezing into the latest, most beautifully designed dress and half starving yourself in order to do so, having just spent a squillion pounds on the latest anti-ageing beauty op, suddenly you find yourself having a natter with Angelina Jolie and getting papped. In the next edition of *Vogue* you see your own stunted frame, dumpy legs, girl-next-door face and 'ordinary' dress next to an actual goddess and want to curl up and die . . . when you are in fact someone like Emily Blunt and unbelievably hot by the standards of all the rest of us.

A GRIT DOCTOR SILVER LINING:

At least we have a shot at looking good at the parties we go to, because thankfully our own circles tend to be comprised of our equals. Angelina Jolie and Emily Blunt types NFI.

And while I'm on the subject, what is going on with that whole 'pillow face' debacle? Why *on earth* would you pay money to make your face fatter? I am in a constant battle to 'de-puffyfy' my pillow face and the idea of paying money to have it injected so it inflates even more flies in the face of common sense to me. Look, I know that as you get old your face gets thinner and so the trick is to puff out the face so that it matches your twelve-year-old's arse. They could not have got this more wrong. In my opinion, one of the few physical benefits to ageing is losing your fat face and seeing your own cheekbones for the first time. And your arse is meant to get bigger (within reason) as you progress through the decades so that it complements your more angular face.

These pillow-faced celebs (who shall remain nameless for legal reasons that no amount of grit doctoring could circumvent) are fighting the battle that cannot be won and losing it with bells on. We can only look on in horror as we watch those faces, frozen in time, puffy and askew and starting to resemble distorted caricatures of their younger selves. The result of age-delay surgery is such an odd look, isn't it? In many cases it is not even remotely attractive. Has it become something else, something much more dangerous and toxic, I wonder; emblematic of a youth which we have come to venerate at all costs, which we equate with power and success? The ridding of any trace of experience, of all lines and texture from these faces screams: 'I WILL NOT CHANGE, I WILL NOT GROW OLD, I AM BETTER THAN THAT.'

Look at Charlotte Rampling or Meryl Streep or Helen Mirren – their beauty is so distinctive *because of*, not in spite of, the fact that it is etched into every one of those lines and every textured nook and cranny. Trying to make ourselves look the same as a million other plastic celebs is robbing us of our own look and distancing us from a vital part of our nature, of who we are. And it looks rubbish anyway.

• The Grit Doctor is all about winning and I cannot see the point in expending energy fighting a losing battle. What a colossal waste of time. We *must* grow old. We *must* decay and sag (within reason). Instead of desperately fighting the superficial indications of our decline, wouldn't it be better to engage in a battle worth winning? After all, no one is going to look at your fave celeb when they are ninety-five and perv over how hot they still are.

We must fight to be as effective as we can be in our lives during the short time available to us. And if we fight hard enough, the impact we make may long outlast our physical selves. We need to shift our focus from looking in the mirror all the time to looking outwards again at the bigger picture. This also has the impact of making us appear a million times more attractive anyway, because your character – what you have stood for in your life and the difference you have made in other people's – will make you a magnet to every person you come into contact with.

THE GRIT DOCTOR SAYS:

Fight for your life not for your looks

And when we feel better about what we are doing with our lives and are so busy making a difference in other people's, we won't even have time to look in the mirror let alone feel depressed about the way we look. The more distance we put between ourselves and a mirror, the more pleasantly surprised we are when we return to it. Another inverse relationship.

THE GRIT DOCTOR SAYS:

It is ugly to care so much about how we look. It is ugly and it makes us *look* ugly too.

Ruth

Just in case you now have a mental image of me as some hairy-armpitted-sandal-wearing-do-gooder who lives in a house without mirrors and spends every waking hour trying to make life better for others – think again. I am as vain and selfish and self-obsessed as the next person. But it really bothers me and I know deep down that I am more at peace with myself when I forget about all that beauty crap and focus my energies on everything else instead. But for the love of God don't beat yourself up thinking I have got any of this shit sorted. Far from it.

 ## NO MORE MIRRORS

Other than getting dressed in the morning and washing your face before bed, let's give up looking in the mirror for a month. And that includes checking out our reflection in shop windows. I wonder how much time this would save and how much happier and prettier we will feel? I'm in, I need the extra time to finish this book anyway.

When it comes to our looks, surely it is all about accepting the ageing process and celebrating the decade we are actually in – not trying desperately to cling on to the previous one. The caveat being that if there are things that are making you unhappy, which can be changed through sensible DIET and EXERCISE, then take the necessary action and stop wasting any more time whingeing about whatever it is not being the way you want it to be.

> 'Do not regret growing older. It is a privilege denied to many.' *Unknown*

The point of this silly table, other than to provide some light relief, is to remind ourselves there are pros and cons to every age. Getting older does not mean that life is over, or that things will never be as good as they were in your rose-tinted youth. My mother always says to me, as her mother used to say to her, 'every age has its compensations'. How right she is. It is our attitude to the decade we are in that needs GYSTing, and not looking through rose-tinted glasses back upon our misspent youth all the time, nor being fearful of the decade that is to come.

THE GRIT DOCTOR SAYS:
The decade just past was every bit as challenging and difficult as the one you are in, so no need to get all nostalgic and misty eyed about its passing any more.

Good things about being in your …	Not-so-good things about being in your …

Twenties

Good things:
- Boundless energy.
- Fry-ups, beer, whatever, makes not a dent in your willowy frame.
- You can do anything, live anywhere – travel abroad and not care about cockroaches, or tomorrow.
- Getting away with being grown-up and deeply immature, all at once.

Not-so-good things:
- Having to share your fridge space with three smelly boys who steal your chocolate.
- Still getting spots.
- Being stranded between childhood and adulthood and not knowing which you'd rather fall into.
- Wondering why you hate your job when it was your 'dream'. And you have no money.

Thirties

Good things:
- Owning up to the fact that you hate clubbing.
- Finally having some disposable income and a car which doesn't fail *every* MOT.
- Realising that it's OK to go and watch *Twilight* on your own, or eat alone in restaurants.
- Children? Maybe.

Not-so-good things:
- Hangovers which now last for more than one day.
- Having to go to weddings *every sodding weekend*.
- Realising the popular fashions of your salad days are now fashionably 'retro'.
- Mortgages
- Grey hairs and lines where there was only smooth baby-skin before.

Forties

Good things:
- Being able to justify health spas and beauty treatments.
- Not having to pretend to be young and enjoying your individuality.
- Watching *Antiques Roadshow* religiously and *without shame*.

Not-so-good things:
- Sparx now essential.
- Realising you are old enough to be your new celeb crush's mother.
- No longer being able to hear conversations in bars due to the *horrifically loud music*.
- Graduating from MILF to cougar.

Fifties

Good things:
- Your children finally being old enough to move out of home.
- Really getting into the 'things aren't the way they used to be' riff.
- Comfy knickers.
- The menopause – goodbye cramps.

Not-so-good things:
- Loss – parents, children leaving home.
- In spite of their 'education', your children still depending on you for financial support.
- The first hair on your chin (not for the GD, sadly) and the worsening effects of gravity.
- The menopause – hot flushes at very inappropriate moments.

Sixties

Good things:
- Giving your grandchildren back at the end of the day.
- Swearing at people without retribution.
- Bus pass and other assorted freebies.
- Realising that there is life after work and adventures are still possible.

Not-so-good things:
- Your wretched children not giving you any grandchildren/too many wretched grandchildren.
- Becoming invisible.
- Everyone (including you) always talking about their aches and pains.

6

STOP TALKING SHIT

Developing a better relationship with the words that come out of your mouth is another *vital skill* in the art of shit togetherness. Powerful people, those whom we admire and respect, are those for whom **what they say and how they then act are consistent with one another**. Think how little respect you may have for David Cameron, for example, but how much for Nelson Mandela. Or, a more relevant example might be the friend you have who is always banging on about some project or another (moving to Italy, getting thin) and who you barely listen to any more, and are certainly not remotely inspired by, because you know one thing for certain: they ain't never gonna do it. This judgement is based on the years and years of experience you have of this person never doing what they say they are going to do. How weak. How lame. It is such a simple thing too, to say what you are going to do and then follow through with it, but it is amazing how often we fall short and how disempowering it is, not just for others who we may have let down but for ourselves.

Our Inner Bitch hates it when we talk shit and so it always causes a degree of anxiety within us, which we try and silence with cake, drink or whatever numbing tool we have to hand. We all do it. And we could all do it a lot less.

SAID IT? DO IT

But how? **Practice. Repetition. Practice. Repetition. Practice. Repetition: HABIT FORMATION.**

Example: 'Honey, I'm going for a run tonight at seven, if that's OK?' (Boyfriend thinking, *She'll never go*, but saying, 'Sure'.) But this time, come 7 p.m., you just go off on your run. No big scene or wild applause, just the simple act of following through on what you said you were going to do.

Similarly, 'Darling, when are you going to build those shelves?' 'I'll do them on Saturday after the football.' (Wife crying inside knowing this means the shelves will not get built.) Think how much more you would respect him if, this time, he got up immediately after the football and calmly built the shelves, without a fuss. It cuts both ways.

This simple act of doing what you said you were going to do *when you said you were going to do it* will have a huge impact on all your relationships, but most importantly on the relationship you have with yourself. It is the beginning of self-respect and trust. You will meet your deadlines and feel good about yourself. Before long people will start to really listen again to what you say, and take what you say very seriously indeed, because you have become a person of your word. This is the first step in taking responsibility for your life and a huge leap forward for shit togetherness.

When you stop talking shit, you will automatically become much more powerful because you will no longer be the sort of person who is willing to say something and then not follow through on it. Not following through makes you weak and unreliable. On the other hand, following through *consistently* on what you say has an immediate and extremely positive impact on your character: it makes you strong, reliable and trustworthy. Honouring your word will make you about a million times more effective and powerful in your life *right now*. It will give you courage and confidence because you know that you will always deliver on your promises. Sounds so very simple and it really is. But to actually *do it successfully* requires a good bit of gristle: the more you flex, the more you answer to your Inner Bitch, the more you beast yourself when you fail – the more powerful and über efficient an operator you will become.

THE GRIT DOCTOR WILL SEE YOU NOW

Q: What do I do when I fail?

A: Apologise, to whoever it is you have let down, or to yourself, and do not give an excuse for the failure. It is not anyone else's fault, nor is it circumstance's fault. It is *your* fault. To avoid unnecessary repeated failures, try to think of all the words that come out of your mouth as promises that you are breaking if you fail to act on them. A great deal of anxiety will be averted if we break

---

fewer promises. It is so simple and so powerful and so within us to cure all at the same time. And it's so basic, it's embarrassing.

SOME HEAVY SHIT

You are what you say every bit as much as what you do. The two are inextricably linked and ought to marry together seamlessly. Your words include *everything* you say: when you are slagging someone off behind their back, or on Twitter, as much as when you are singing someone's praises. Whatever words you utter, both spoken and written, you must be responsible for. Adopting a more powerful relationship with the words you say will make you think much more carefully before you open your mouth. And this is a very good thing indeed.

THE GRIT DOCTOR SAYS:
Actions speak louder than words but YOUR WORD BACKED UP BY RELEVANT ACTION IS THE LOUDEST.

THE *SHIT* LAWYER

As a criminal barrister, I was surrounded by so much bullshit and legal jargon that I have become something of an expert at detecting, in both myself and others, even the faintest whiff of waffle. Waffle is one of the arch-enemies of shit togetherness. The art of clear speech and clear written language is a key skill to develop in the pursuit of a better life. Why? Because it is only when we are crystal clear in what we say and think that we are able to express ourselves fully and our actions become relevant and consistent with our goals. Paring down our thinking and use of language – by eliminating waffle – ultimately leads to a paring down of our actions, which results in getting more shit done in less time. Bingo.

No one is more guilty of word play than the 'professionals', and lawyers are the worst culprits. I have an ongoing joke with my sister, who is currently training to be a barrister, about how much this goes on in a criminal court and how much time is wasted as a result. My sister is a master of getting shit done and cannot bear the prevarication that surrounds her job. Perhaps it is because lawyers are relied on as 'experts' that we somehow feel a need to obfuscate matters in order for others to think they need us in the first place! My sister reported this to me the other day on a trial in which she was taking notes:*

Ahem. Just writing about the law has caused me to slip back into waffle mode: prevarication; obfuscate . . . I shall desist forthwith.

Submission: May it please Your Honour [*totally unnecessary ass kissing*], I would like to take this opportunity to make Your Honour aware [*far too many words to say something very simple*] that over the luncheon [*who the feck calls it luncheon?*] adjournment, I will be considering my position as to whether or not to make an application to stay proceedings [*translation: I might ask you to stop the case*].

Warning the judge about an application that may or may not be made is completely unnecessary. Either make it or shut up.

The moral of the tale is, if your gran wouldn't get it, you need to be clearer. And, if you can say it in one word rather than three, use one. Fewer words spoken take less time to say. If you are *talking* nonsense you are *thinking* nonsense and vice versa and it is all eating into your twenty-four hours. Clean it all up. Give your brain a really good wash. How? Listen to The GD and then start answering to your own IB. She never waffles and she speaks in very clear language.

THE GRIT DOCTOR SAYS:

Brainwashing is the answer.

LISTEN UP

Talking clearly is incredibly important: it is a skill we can all spend our lives honing. Listening, however, is every bit as important in terms of GYST. There is nothing more attractive than someone who really listens; not pretends to listen (guys, take note here) which is the worst kind of listening, nor listens in the 'I know better' kind of way where you can't wait to get your penny's-worth of advice in and so are only listening for an opportunity in which to give it, or in the sort of 'autobiographical' way which is only listening to find a pause in which you can then give your bigger, better story. This isn't going to help. The best sort of listening is just to shut the f**k up and listen properly. I cannot put it any plainer than that. Hear what the person is saying by being present, concentrate on the words coming out of their mouth – don't think about what's on telly tonight, or work or whatever else, but actually listen to what is being said . . . and not to what you think they *really mean* either. It is a beautiful thing to do: it is free, it makes you *so* much more powerful and makes the sharer feel that what they have to say is important, which creates a really great space for a conversation. This is something worth practising: not listening out for anything except the words coming out of their mouth.

Try it out: There will be someone in your life who you always listen to through the same filter. Husbands, boyfriends, girlfriends, best friends, mothers, fathers, annoying brothers. The filter ensures that you listen for the story you have created about your relationship with them and as a result, often get unnecessarily upset. For example:

> Mum *asks*: Darling, when will you be coming home for Christmas?
> Daughter *hears*: You are so inconsiderate. So and so's daughter *always* comes home for Christmas. *And she has a baby.*

Let's review the evidence: *She asked a perfectly innocent question and you made the rest up.* Be conscious that the filter is there and try to have an honest conversation, where you are listening from a completely neutral position – this can really freshen up a tired relationship. Anyway, aren't you bored with being so irritated by your friend/husband/mother/sister all the time? If so, nothing to lose from trying it out . . .

THE GRIT DOCTOR WILL SEE YOU NOW

Q: Why is this important?

A: DOH. Because it is only when we listen properly that we can actually hear what is being said.

7

CIRCUMSTANTIAL
EVIDENCE

One of the big errors we make, one of the things responsible for our sense of inertia when it comes to making significant changes in our lives, is the misconception that we need something else to happen first. That we need to understand something about ourselves, or that we need other things to be in order, or specific events to have taken place, before we can make our first move. This approach is paralysing because it will always leave us at the mercy of our circumstances. It allows circumstances to dictate the actions we take and the choices we make, which is incredibly limiting when you pause to reflect upon it.

As we have established (but it bears repeating here), The Grit Doctor Way is to take the reverse position: action comes first and in taking action stuff gets worked out along the way. Do something, take action, and your life begins to take shape. It is an attitude that puts all the power back into our hands because we can all take some action, no matter what else is going on in our lives or however bad we may be feeling at the time. It is something we all have control over and can all be masters of, and as an attitude to life it sure as shit beats living at the mercy of someone or something else all the time.

The kicker, of course, is that in adopting this powerful *I am in charge of my life* stance, it means you have to give up the *I am a victim of my circumstances* position. When you are in charge and you are calling the shots **the buck stops with you.** Powerful, yes, but intimidating too because it shifts all the responsibility onto your shoulders. You lose the safety net that circumstantial evidence has provided, as you are no longer going to be blaming anyone or anything but yourself for your life being the way that it is.

THE GRIT DOCTOR SAYS:

Leave your circumstances at the door.

WHAT IS SHE TALKING ABOUT?

Circumstances are things like:

- Crap parents

- Your flat on the top floor of a housing estate with no lift

- Being a skint single mum

- Your husband leaving you for another woman

- Your dog dying

The gritty truth is that circumstances can become excuses that we all rely on to avoid getting shit done. Any sentence that comes out of your mouth, or simply gets an airing in your head, which begins with the words, 'I can't because . . .' *has got to go.* These circumstantial excuses are preventing you from getting your shit together because they are immovable things that you cannot immediately change and so continue to safely hide behind, telling yourself that if only your circumstances were different, you would be able to do X, Y and Z. This is really only ever an excuse to avoid taking any action. And yes, I am talking about the really tragic stuff here: death included. Acknowledging the pain of these experiences is an essential part of the grieving process but wallowing in the pain to the extent that these experiences dictate the course of your life is not. *Pain is as necessary to a good life as everything else* and is not to be used as a reason for your shit being all over the place any more. Life is hard. Suck it up.

This position, when Grit Doctored, becomes something over which you suddenly have a great deal of potential power. Do X, Y and Z, no matter what the circumstances may be. This approach may ultimately result in a shift in your unfavourable circumstances as well. So it's win, WIN.

THE BLAME GAME

Circumstances become particularly problematic in the context of GYST when we blame them for our lives not being the way we want them to be and convince ourselves that there is nothing we can do about it. A lot of us get stuck because we are caught up in blaming *other people* as well as *other things* for everything. We blame the weather for stopping us going outside to exercise and forcing us to retreat to the sofa with a chocolate bar; our badly paid jobs and sky-high rents for making us poor; our parents for making us unhappy. Whatever it is, when we are blaming someone or something else for our lives being a certain way, we are without doubt shooting ourselves in the proverbial foot.

If there was one thing I could change about the world it would be that every person take responsibility for themselves and their actions, or their inaction. It is that big. No matter how awful the tragedies, how bad the parenting, how tempting the chocolate, until we own it all, until we say *I have a choice* and refuse to be beaten by the sadness – no matter how profound – by the shit that has happened or has not happened, by the loves and friendships lost, by the shitty boss, by the not winning the lottery – yet – we will never begin to see what we are capable of. Because remaining in the blame game is a form of forced self-imprisonment. We are chained to it, to the certainty of it, to the idea that because of A, B is always a given and that what we really want is somehow always out of our reach.

THE GRIT DOCTOR SAYS:

Who you are is NEVER your circumstances.

I am writing this during the 2012 Paralympics. Every time I switch on the television, there's another wonderful example of an athlete who has refused to let their circumstances defy them. Take Martine Wright – she was running late for work, having been out with colleagues the night before celebrating London's successful Olympics bid. It was 7 July 2005. She was travelling on the train to Aldgate that was bombed. Her journey that day caused her to lose both legs, eighty per cent of her blood and her life as she knew it. After the physical and mental agony of rehabilitation and learning to walk on prosthetics, she quit her job, fought for a public inquiry into 7/7, earned her pilot's licence in South Africa, married her husband, Nick, and gave birth. Then she became a Paralympian.

> 'There was nothing that I could have done to stop what happened that day, it was going to happen and it was going to happen because – maybe – I was always meant to be where I am today.' *Martine Wright*

Not only does Martine not blame her circumstances for any-thing, *she owns her circumstances, she chooses them.* She has adopted a position which frees her to say, 'This is who I am and what was always meant to be. I was always meant to be a Paralympian.' And really it is just that: a point of view. An overwhelmingly humbling and inspiring one – but a point of view all the same. She could have chosen the point of view that said, 'Why me? Why has this happened to me? My life is over.' And had she done so, I wonder, where would she be now? Both are entirely valid positions to adopt from that set of circumstances, one free-ing, liberating and positive, the other not. What happened was that she was bombed and lost both her legs. How she chose to see it, *what she chose to make it mean for her*, was entirely her own business.

Choosing the circumstances of your life *no matter how diffi-cult they may be* is always the answer. It requires an incredible amount of courage and strength to say 'I choose no legs'. Pause. Breathe. Read it again. 'I choose no legs'. This moves me beyond measure.

STORY TELLING

A friend of mine was engaged to be married to the love of his life. Invitations had gone out, dresses and suits were bought, flowers chosen ... and he was jilted – not quite at the altar

Four Weddings-style, but a few weeks before. Awful, yes, but this story, this one event, became the story of his life. It was the story he told everybody when he'd had a glass of wine, it was the story that informed his view of *all* women, and his choices in relationships were based on this story, and formed the backbone of who he was, who he was *choosing* to be. If it were only a story that stayed in fantasy land that would be fine, but it was actually really toxic and dangerous precisely because it *didn't* remain in fantasy land at all – it became his truth.

If you repeat 'the story' – whatever it is – often enough, both to yourself and to others, adding embellishments along the way, it gathers momentum and power until the story owns you, it dictates the decisions and choices you make. If your point of view is all men are scum, sure enough, all the men you meet will prove you right. We are so hell bent on being right that we simply gather evidence that supports our point of view and blindly ignore anything that contradicts it. Life will always be how you declare it to be. It is always just so. 'All men are scum.' Sure they are. 'We never have any money.' Sure we don't. 'My husband never listens to me.' Of course he doesn't. 'I don't have time.' No you don't. It is always how we say it is.

'It is my daily mood that makes the weather.
I possess tremendous power to make life miserable

or joyous. I can be a tool of torture or an instrument of inspiration, I can humiliate or humour, hurt or heal. In all situations, it is my response that decides whether a crisis is escalated or de-escalated, and a person is humanised or de-humanised.' *J. W. Goethe*

THE GRIT DOCTOR SAYS:

What really matters is not *what happened* BUT YOUR RESPONSE TO IT.

THE *SHIT* LAWYER

I used to spend a lot of time dealing with circumstantial evidence. For example: a murder is committed. A can of Coke is found yards from the scene of the crime, spattered in blood. Under forensic examination, it is found to contain the DNA of the murder victim and that of the accused. Depending on whether I was prosecuting or defending the case, that piece of circumstantial evidence would have a completely different story attached to it. *The same piece of evidence – depending on the story you have to tell – takes on a completely different complexion.* In the prosecution case, the can of Coke irrefutably shows the accused to be the murderer, given that both his blood *and* that of the victim were found on it at the murder scene; in the defence case, it is simply a discarded item of drink from an innocent member of the public with a tiny cut on his finger, who was in the wrong place at the wrong time.

A GRIT DOCTOR CONFESSION:
The closest I ever got to an *actual* murder case during my time at the criminal bar was listening transfixed while my husband talked about *his* cases.

The danger with circumstantial evidence is that it gathers strength the more story we add to it. Using the barrister analogy, we were always taught that circumstantial evidence, on its own, was potentially very weak, but if there were several strands of circumstantial evidence that could be joined together, then that weak, stringy piece of evidence would gradually change into tightly woven rope and could become very powerful evidence indeed. Think of the first thin strand as *the bad thing that happened* (I got dumped). The other strands might be: all men are scum; I am ugly; the world is bad . . . in our evidence-gathering mission we will always find our story perfectly supported and the rope woven tighter and tighter, becoming harder and harder to break.

That is, until we Grit Doctor it: we can break the rope once we are able to see it all as a story that we made up and can just as easily give up and throw away.

 **BE A *SHIT* LAWYER**

If you think you might have been using circumstantial evidence to create your own story, have a go at this exercise. I want you to create a story from the opposite point of view, so you are Grit Doctoring your position – make up a story that forces you to see the exact same evidence from another angle. Create the most convincing case you can to prosecute your real-life story, based on exactly the same evidence. Make the best possible argument you can for it and then don an imaginary wig and gown and make your closing speech to a pretend jury. When you are finished (and the jury return and are unanimously in favour of your arguments), make that your last ever speech/story.

THE GRIT DOCTOR ASKS:

If you can convince a jury of the opposite of
what you really believe, using the identical set of
circumstances, then surely the time has come to
give up the story?

'People are always blaming their circumstances for
what they are. I don't believe in circumstances.
The people who get on in this world are the people
who get up and look for the circumstances they
want, and, if they can't find them, make them.'
George Bernard Shaw

Think how much power we would automatically shift our way
if we chose to accept the circumstances of our lives as they are,
and stopped resisting them or wishing they were different or
gave up creating stories around them. When we quietly accept
them, circumstances begin to lose their power as we start to
believe that they can't in fact control our destinies unless we
allow them to – that they do not, in fact, have anything to do
with who or what we are. They are merely circumstances.
George Bernard Shaw was telling us to take back the power
from our circumstances.

149

THE GRIT DOCTOR SAYS:

You are the architect of your life, you make it interesting, you create it. You. You is what needs to happen, not anything else.

All well and good, but how?

THE GRIT DOCTOR SAYS:

Stop whingeing about your circumstances all the time and using them as an excuse for not doing shit, for starters.

THE GRIT DOCTOR WILL SEE YOU NOW

Q. I am in a *really* difficult situation though. I am a single mum, living on the top floor of a tower block with a broken lift. My mum looks after my little girl while I work part time in the local super-market. I really want to be a teacher, but I feel as though it's impossible.

A. Almost anything is possible if you are willing to break the project down into shelves and are committed to the end goal. Using The GYST Facilitator, you need to identify the first steps in your quest, decide on a timeframe and get cracking without further ado. Find out who is responsible for the maintenance of the lift, phone them and get it sorted. There may be financial support/bursaries/childcare benefits available to you should you enrol on a teacher-training course, so perhaps looking into those would be an early shelf. You have been able to keep a part-time job despite these difficult circumstances, and there is no reason why you can't retrain as a teacher too. I'm not saying it will be easy, but you absolutely can do it if you are committed and willing to put the work in. And just think, once you do qualify and have a teaching job, that might be your ticket out of the tower block and into a ground-floor flat and a brighter future for you and your daughter.

THE GRIT DOCTOR INSTRUCTS:
BIN YOUR CIRCUMSTANCES and embrace the principle of BEING IN ACTION. Being in action, no matter what the circumstances of your life may be, is an attitude that makes us free.

It will make you feel good – really good – to get stuff done again and to succeed, whatever else may be going on in your life that is difficult; whatever tragedy, whatever disaster – no matter how big or small – that you have been using as the 'reason' you can't learn to swim/get a new job/repaint the kitchen/stop bickering with your husband/take your daughter to the park/sign up for a Pilates class/stand up to your boss (delete/add as appropriate).

GRIT DOCTOR TRANSLATION:

'Reason' is code for 'excuse'.

MAGIC AND CHANCE: A GRIT DOCTOR CURVEBALL

While I am an advocate of being incredibly organised and somewhat ruthless in terms of time management, it must never be at the expense of the 'magic' in life. By magic, I mean the possibilities created by randomness, by chance encounters and the unseen forces outside of our control. Serendipity. It is always easy in retrospect, when describing a success story, to find it explained without reference to anything but hard work and the 'gifts' of the people involved ... but the magic was invariably present somewhere, and more often than not was crucial to the success of the thing.

We need to be open to these magical moments: these are the opportunities not labelled 'Opportunity', when something in your brain just clicks, or you suddenly have an idea just by looking at something. Harnessing that is Grit Gold, but it is, of course, meaningless unless you are able to both recognise it and exploit it.

THE GRIT DOCTOR WILL SEE YOU NOW

Q: What on earth is she talking about?

A: It happens all the time: the business idea that you shared over a pint on Friday night, which your mates shot down in flames and trampled all over, or the idea of emigrating to Australia that your father squished when you mentioned it ... and the magic was lost.

WHERE THE MAGIC IS CONCERNED THE GOLDEN RULES ARE:

1. DON'T SHARE.
2. Follow that grinstinct through into ACTION.

You do not need the approval of others. Nothing is more likely to guarantee you don't follow through on an idea than sharing about it when it is in its most fragile, almost enbryonic state. You may as well shit on it. Quite literally. The time for sharing or getting others to bring their magic to the table (or calling a VSSC member) is later, once you have already begun the project, got a business plan and investors, or written a synopsis and a couple of chapters, or tailored your CV to the job application. Just get the ball rolling and create it yourself. There will be plenty of time to talk about it when it's done or while you are *actually doing it*.

The magic doesn't just apply to genius business ideas, it is also about cultivating your curious side and following through on it. And it applies to everything that interests you, to the detail of life and to nature. If you are fascinated by birds, follow up on it, explore your interest. Get curious. My husband is a master of this art – his curiosity knows no bounds. And it is a beautiful quality shared by all his family. I am convinced it is the primary reason that they are all such lovely people. They are fascinated by life and are always following through on things that intrigue them. Not, it has to be said, in a commercial sense. But they are none the poorer for it. Their lives are rich and abundant because they are forever looking outside of themselves and are constantly surprised by the beauty and wonder of life. And they all love reading. A lot. Getting buried in a good book is a wonderful antidote to sadness or loneliness. And the same applies to whatever turns you on. The key is to bury yourself in it: birds, films, books, art, music, theatre, sex, running!

THE GRIT DOCTOR SAYS:

Get buried.

PART 3

SPIRIT

8

LOVE THY NEIGHBOUR

Love thy neighbour as thyself. This is a central tenet of Christianity, but the concept of reciprocity, of 'do unto others as you would have them do unto you', is found in all of the world's major religions. But whether or not you believe in God, or any other deity or deities, whatever your religious or anti-religious persuasion, you can still make this simple concept a central part of your life. If we all took on this golden rule, and tried to practise it daily, just imagine the sort of world we would inhabit.

At its core, it is about putting love where there is none. Thy neighbour may be George Osborne, we must still love him. 'Thy neighbour' is *everybody* we come into contact with, and all those we don't but whose lives our actions affect: the bus driver, the cashier at Tesco, your daughter's teacher, your husband, your mother, the nurse who cares for your grandfather with Alzheimer's, the Queen herself. We are commanded to treat all of them as we would like to be treated ourselves, *with the same love and respect.*

This is, of course, impossible.

But that doesn't mean we can't try, that we can't have a shot, that we can't hold it up as the ideal to which we will constantly aspire. In practice, on an average day in my life, it might look like this:

- Smiling to the twins first thing in the morning and giving them, and Olly, hugs and kisses and telling them all how much I love them – even if the twins have kept me up all night.

- Taking time to talk to the cashier in Sainsbury's and ask her how her day is going.

- Paying my bills on time.

- Not complaining about anything or anybody to anyone.

- Not judging the weird builder up the road who keeps looking at me when I walk by.

- Not slagging anyone off behind their back.

- *Listening* to my mother when she phones (see page 135).

- Taking time to phone my grandmother, or sister or brothers, and reconnecting with them and their lives.

It is hardest to do this with those closest to us, which is why it is *essential* to practise on these very people. There is absolutely no point in practising on the Queen or the person you fancy or the boss you are trying to persuade to promote you. Because it is incredibly easy to put our best foot forward in all those circumstances. Grit Doctor it: make it really difficult, and get more mileage out of your practice by trying it out on your other half when they are at their most irritating, on your toddler after another sleepless night, or on the person to whom you are always rude or short, or who you are constantly complaining about. Because they are the ones who get all of our shit thrown over them on a daily basis. It is time to start cleaning it up. It can be done. We just need to keep trying. And it is so important that we do because, like cleaning our homes physically, and talking less shit, we need to work on improving our behaviour. Little shifts can have seismic impacts.

> 'Where there is no love, put love, and you will draw love out.' *St John Of The Cross*

 AN EXERCISE FOR GRIT DODGERS: SMILE AT STRANGERS

Grit Doctor caveat: there is an art to this that takes it from being totally deranged to positively uplifting for the recipient. Practice is the only way forward and will take you from rictus grin to natural, dazzling smile. You know you are getting better at it when people smile back rather than: a) run away crying; b) stare at you quizzically with furrowed brow, trying to figure out how they know you; or c) slap you in the face. If c) happens, do be sure to turn the other cheek . . .

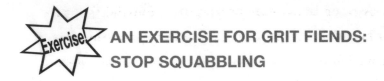
⭐ Exercise! AN EXERCISE FOR GRIT FIENDS: STOP SQUABBLING

Squabbling (n.): Meaningless, pointless arguing for the sake of arguing because you are in a bad mood and want to unload shit somewhere.*

Give up squabbling with your other half. In other words, *choose* not to squabble. When you fail, give it up all over again. And again. And again. And again. Forgive yourself for failing and try again.

THE GRIT DOCTOR WARNS:
Bickering and squabbling are the foundation stones upon which divorces are built.

Your other half is the person you have chosen to share your life with. Consider that sentence for a moment and repeat it to yourself. They are the person *you have chosen to spend your life with*. And more than that, they are the *only person you have chosen to spend your life with*. You didn't get to choose your parents, your

*A Grit Doctor definition. Not approved by the OED.

brother or sister or batty aunt or grandad. You didn't even choose your kids. All that consideration we brought to the table and all that we fell in love with, all those qualities that, combined, put them so far above *any other person in the whole world.* The union was as inescapable and inevitable as the gritmin we face on a daily basis and yet ... we all fall into some terrible habits. At best we take them for granted and don't show our love. At worst, we shout and blame them for our life not being the way we want it to be. Isn't it awful? Let's just stop doing it. END. OF.

When in a bickering state of mind, cure yourself by going for a mood-healing run instead. If running's not your bag, do something else distracting, or soothing, instead. Take a bath, go for a walk, go and stand in the garden, jump up and down and scream, and then come back inside again with a fresh perspective. The key is to do something else, anything else but squabble. There are some who swear by a huge fight to clear the air and my view is, it sure as shit beats low-level squabbling ad infinitum. Far better to have the odd blow-out screaming match – and the ensuing endorphin rush from kissing and making up – than a constant turgid bickering dynamic. A full-blown row can help clear the air and, after the dust has settled, you are free to start afresh.

A GRIT DOCTOR RANT

This is slightly off-topic, but ... **no effing date nights when you are married**. YOU CANNOT DATE YOUR SPOUSE. Friday night 'date night' makes me feel sick to the core. Go out together, but stop pretending it's a date. The best bit about a date was that you didn't know how the night was going to end and could get blind drunk and dance until 3 a.m. because you didn't have to get up at the crack of dawn to breastfeed. However, you know very well how a night out with your husband is going to end and it is *not* on the dancefloor of some crazy nightclub or swinging from the chandelier of a Mayfair mansion (entirely fictitious, not a real memory, you understand). It's an enormous achievement just to organise a babysitter and manage to get out of the house wearing something other than your trackie bums and without flecks of baby vom on your face. So don't pile on the added pressure of it being a 'date' night. I was never a fan of dates and consider it to be a major perk of being married that I no longer have to go on any. Rant over.

DO UNTO *ALL* OTHERS

A great deal of stress and anxiety arises from the gap between who we are and who we present to the world, by which I mean how we behave at home and how we behave when we step out of the front door. The most contented people are those for whom very little, if any, gap exists between the two. By contrast, the most deranged types are the ones who behind closed doors are prone to being positively satanic and yet are charm personified around everybody else. They are exhausting themselves being faux kind at work so there is nothing left in the tank to be polite and considerate back at home. The way to address this is not to start being a mega beeyatch out of the home as well, just to balance things out. It is instead to practise being polite, kind, courteous and considerate indoors to those you love the most but who you are most likely to snap at. Like anything, rudeness is simply a bad habit, possibly picked up from the example set by our parents (but we disregard shit like this from now on). In exercising our simple choice *not to do it any more* and backing it up with regular practice, we will be well on our way.

THE GRIT DOCTOR WILL SEE YOU NOW

Q: How does The Grit Doctor know so much about this?

A: Because I am one of the worst culprits for 'at home rudeness' and 'at party charm' and I am *determined* to put a stop to it. This is what I have been doing and I find it has been working wonders: before I snap or say anything mean to Olly or the

---

twins, I take a deep breath, close my eyes instead and do one of the following (just one is usually sufficient to act as a weakness decoy and prevent me descending into verbal meltdown):

- Imagine we were to die in a tragic accident tonight. Is my criticism or complaint necessary, considering we will be dead in a few hours' time?
- Channel my Inner Bitch – the GD – and whatever it was I was about to say in anger, turn it against myself remembering the 'splinter and plank' analogy from my Catechism days. (*And why do you look at the splinter in your brother's eye, but do not consider the plank in your own eye?*) For the benefit of non-Catholics, this translates into: 'You are far from perfect, Ruth'.
- Crack a gag, ideally at my own expense, and make us laugh instead.

Ruth

I literally love my neighbours. Honestly, I cannot believe my luck. Two women, both married with toddlers, who would have been my best mates at school if I'd been lucky enough to meet them. It is heaven to have people like that – in the same boat – only a stone's throw away from my front door. And my next-door neighbour is a wonderful Irish woman who has just turned eighty and is like a surrogate grandmother to me and surrogate great-grandmother to the twins. She kisses their feet in the buggy every time we run into each other on the street and she keeps a set of my keys for when I get locked out of the house – which obviously never happens. Ahem. When I was heading over to Ireland on a promotional tour for RFBR, she slipped a note through my door informing me that her niece lived in Dublin and would be in touch. I had no idea whatsoever how this was going to pan out, but the niece texted me and arranged to pick me up from a book signing at Eason's, after which she took me under her wing on a tour of the sights, via her fabulous pad and much champagne, and then on an incredible night out: dinner, dancing, the whole shebang. I hadn't danced since my wedding day and I had so much fun that night, and she introduced me to some lovely people. I met a guy who has since organised an event and flown me back to Dublin to speak at it! It was the best night out I'd had since having the twins and it all came about because I made friends with an eighty-year-old woman who lives next door.

GRUDGE MATCH

While we are in the spirit of holiness, having taken on the golden rule of doing unto others, I want you to piggyback on the rush of love you are feeling for everybody around you and tackle a biggie that, if it applies to you, is undoubtedly standing in the way of GYST. If you are holding a grudge of any kind, whether you've held it for ten years or a few days, and no matter how big or small you consider it to be, it is holding you back. It is preventing you from fulfilling your GYST potential because it is eating away at your energy levels. The way to get over it is to simply get over it. Call the person in question, or meet up with them (no, emailing doesn't count), say sorry and *give up having to be right about it.* Where has being right got you so far? Nowhere. Give it up. Say sorry, even if you *are* right, and make up. You will feel light as a feather, your face will unfurrow and you will have an injection of energy to start tackling other stuff.

Because grudges act as motivation killers and gristle sappers. They rob you of your GYST mojo, like an insidious poison. Deny it as much as you like, or insist that *your* grudge is an exception, but it ain't. A grudge is a grudge is a grudge – in The Grit Doctor's eyes, they all have the same shape and they all stink. Look at it this way, how has keeping your grudge served you in your life so far? How is the grudge making you feel good about stuff, energising you? Has anything good ever come from bearing this grudge – *ever* – other than being right? No doubt about it, holding on to this grudge is handicapping you from GYST. And you may have lost a really good friend or relative along the way.

THE GRIT DOCTOR SAYS:

BEING RIGHT IS MASSIVELY OVERRATED.

Ruth

My editor forced me to share this story, after she heard me speak about it on the John Murray radio show in Ireland recently. For many years, I held a massive grudge that was totally disproportionate to the harm inflicted or imagined upon me, as is often the case. I was a student barrister living with two great pals from school in a flat owned by the grandmother of one of them. We were paying nominal rent for huge bedrooms in a very central location in London, so we were incredibly lucky. The granddaughter decided to go off travelling (and, by the way, it was on the back of a bus in a remote part of South America that she met her future husband — a great example of 'the magic' in action), leaving me and my mate in the flat. The grandmother decided, without much warning, to boot us out. My mate was OK as she was about to move in with her boyfriend, but skint, single me was not. I was LIVID as I had nowhere to go and was not earning any money. I blamed my friend for not having sorted this all out before she left, but I just let it fester and never confronted her about it. I never told her how I was feeling, I just unceremoniously cut her off by never responding to emails and thinking to myself, *What a bitch to leave me destitute.*

It was about six years later that she got married (goodness me, maybe it was more like ten) and I went to her wedding in Scotland, having softened my stance somewhat on account of robust advice from the other flatmate, who pointed out what an utter twat I was being. Of course what happened wasn't her fault, but I was so obsessed with being righteous and indignant and hard done by that I was blinded by the poison that carrying a grudge generates. As soon as I said sorry I felt a million times better about everything – a heavy feeling left my body and all was well again in my world. An instant injection of good feeling and positive energy to put into taking action elsewhere in my life. And I had a good friend back in my life again, someone whom the grudge-carrying had poisoned me into believing I didn't need or miss.

In saying sorry I was simultaneously taking responsibility for what had happened and letting go of the story I had made up about it *all being someone else's fault.* You may think that my grudge was relatively insignificant but remember that a grudge is a grudge is a grudge. It is true that the bigger the grudge, and the longer it has been held, the greater its poisonous effects and the more it is robbing you of all that fuel to help fire up the rest of your life – but small grudges, slights and imagined insults can fester just as badly. When you give up a *really big* grudge you are going to enjoy an even bigger sense of freedom and release and an enormous injection of fresh energy and motivation. So, what are you waiting for?

'Forgiveness is the key to action
and freedom.' *Hannah Arendt*

IT'S TIME TO GIVE UP HAVING TO BE RIGHT

Let's try to give up having to be right about everything, and be flexible instead – be open to persuasion and to changing our beliefs and ideas. It is surely a much more interesting and exciting way to live, one that opens us up to learning so much more from other people. One of the most limiting things we can say about ourselves or the human condition is that people don't change, that they can't change. How absurd! We can change whenever we want to simply by choosing to. We are not stuck in a certain way of being or limited by the gifts we were or were not born with. We can do almost anything we set our minds to, providing we are willing to take the action necessary and are committed to hard work.

> 'Everything seems impossible until it is done.'
> *Nelson Mandela*

 ## CLEANING UP GRUDGES: AN EXERCISE FOR GRIT FIENDS AND GRIT DODGERS ALIKE

Call everyone you know and tell them you love them, and say sorry for any niggling shit that is in the air between you and infecting your relationship. This includes big and baby grudges alike. A baby grudge might involve your brother who irritated you recently, as a result of which you haven't called him for a week. Call him up, say sorry and put it behind you. A biggie might involve your alcoholic mother who was hopeless, and still is, and whom you resent intensely and have spent your whole life blaming for the fact that you have a shit job and no boyfriend. Call her up, say sorry and put it behind you. Gritty? Yes; a really big deal? Yes; impossible? *NO*.

THE GRIT DOCTOR WILL SEE YOU NOW

Q: Why should I say sorry when I'm not? I have *nothing* to be sorry for – it's her who needs to apologise.

A: Don't question the logic. Just act. Start the conversation without blame or judgement, from a place of love and forgiveness, and who knows where it will lead? Beats the same old, same old sadness and resentment and bitterness, surely? It will generate hope and with any luck take the relationship to a better place. *Be the bigger person. Say sorry. Even when it is not your fault. It is so much easier than you think.* Go on, I dare you.

9

GREEN GRASS THINKING

Oh, do look how lush, how green, how verdant, how much more abun-
dant the grass is over there! In *her* career. In *his* relationship. In *their*
home. Sound familiar? We are all guilty of this 'the grass is
greener' thinking, and it is entirely pointless and defeatist. Why?
Because the green grass is an ever-movable feast. Once you step
over the fence into the lush pasture you've been admiring for so
long, you will find that it is in fact exactly the same colour as the
field you have left. When you look back from the new pasture
into your old, recently vacated patch, well, what do you know?
It is so very green and verdant and lush. Wouldn't you be happier just over there?

THE PERVERSITY OF GGT IN ACTION

Person A and Person B are the same age and work in the same
industry.

Person A works hard but isn't paid overtime, so unless
absolutely necessary she doesn't stay late or work weekends. She
likes clothes, going out and nice holidays and gets into debt
during her twenties. She does well at work, is promoted every

few years and continues to enjoy her job. In her mid-twenties she starts renting a studio flat, which means she doesn't have much spare cash to put away – especially once she's bought a few new items from Topshop and paid for that minibreak to Amsterdam. Career-wise, she is doing fine and is on a par with others her age. She enjoys her job, has good friends and a busy social life. She is single, although she goes on lots of dates, and has no savings.

Person B works evenings and weekends and quickly gains a reputation for going the extra mile. She is rapidly promoted. She often turns down invites because she'd rather stay at the office; she sits at her desk to eat a lunch she's brought from home. She is incredibly careful with her money and saves a proportion of her salary every month. Once a year she has a big, expensive holiday but this is her only major indulgence. She lives in a cheap room in a shared house throughout her twenties. She gets into a serious relationship in her late twenties and is engaged by the time she's thirty. She is managing a large team and has a very impressive salary – which together with her savings allows her to put a deposit on a house and pay for a lavish wedding.

Person A looks at Person B and wishes she'd worked harder, been more prudent and thinks she must be less talented.

Person B looks at Person A and wishes she'd had more fun, worn shorter skirts while she still could and thinks she must be really boring.

Who you most identify with in the above scenario may reveal something about your choices in life and where the grass always looks greener to you. It's easy to spot why Person A hasn't achieved as much as Person B in her life, but also not difficult to imagine why Person B might feel a tiny bit jealous of Person A's footloose-and-fancy-free existence. Person B is clearly GYSTful and Person A could *arguably* do with taking a leaf out of her book. However, we never *really* know the truth of a person's life. Both Person A and Person B have made their choices and could, in reality, feel any of the following about them: a) gloriously happy; b) desperately miserable; or c) a bit 'meh'. The reality is we will never know.

So *banish* GGT once and for all, say I. If you want what someone else has, then the time has come to wake up and smell the coffee. Stop being envious of the end product and start making better friends with all the hard graft that lies behind it. And for the record, neither Person A or B is better or worse. They are the same.

THE GRIT DOCTOR SAYS:

Green Grass Thinking is another mode of being that prevents us from embracing and enjoying the life we actually have, with all the choices we have made and the relationships that really matter to us.

 **TENDING TO YOUR OWN LAWN**

Stand on your own patch of grass (it doesn't have to be *actual* grass) and repeat the following: THE GRASS IS GREEN ENOUGH HERE. THE GRASS IS GREEN ENOUGH HERE. THE GRASS IS GREEN ENOUGH HERE.

Ignore the fact that the patch is in fact brown, uneven and far from healthy. Close your eyes if necessary and visualise the greenest grass you have ever seen right there under your own two feet, where you live. Now is not the time to start whingeing about not having a garden or any outdoor space. The exercise works just as well in your living room or bedroom. Close your eyes and *just imagine*. Take a deep breath, picture the beautiful green lawn, smell it, own it. *Oh dear, is that a steamy brown turd I can smell?* (*Opens one eye to confirm presence*) *Yes! And I love it all.*

THERE IS NO GREENER GRASS ANYWHERE ELSE. THE GRASS IS *GREEN ENOUGH* WHERE I AM.

The inherent problem with GGT is that it traps us in wanting someone else's life and distracts us from being present to the joy in our own. Every life, no matter how enviable it looks to you from the other side of the fence, has its difficulties, its compromises, its pros and cons.

THE GRIT DOCTOR SAYS:

All the grass is the same colour. It is the lens through which you see it that alters its shade.

Ruth

I have so many conversations with other mums who, when they find out that I'm a writer, say: 'I wish I could write a book. I would have a much better work–life balance – looking after the babies, working from home, it's perfect!' I am always quick to point out the downsides: no adult interaction, maddening constant internal dialogue, lack of structure, having to generate everything from within my own head at a kitchen table, irregular and unstable income. I really ham it up too, so that I hopefully dispel any more Green Grass Thinking. And what I wouldn't give some days for a regular nine-to-five, to be back in my wig and gown giving a speech to a jury, to have that sense of accomplishment, triumph even, when the verdict goes my way, for after-work drinks, for office shenanigans and politics, for being part of something bigger, for structure and organisation, for a desk! But look, I love what I have chosen to do because I choose to love it. Every job, every relationship, every work–life balancing/juggling act has its challenges. The key is finding the one which suits you well enough and accepting in the process that it is never going to be perfect. Not anywhere near perfect.

THE GRIT DOCTOR SAYS:

Life is not just imperfect, it is a grit sandwich and the more grit you are willing to eat, the better life starts to taste.

HOW DO I JUDGE IF MY JOB IS *GOOD ENOUGH*?

Do you:

- Spend every Sunday night crying about the prospect of having to go to work and need to take anti-anxiety meds just to cope?

- Play EuroMillions religiously every week, buy scratch-cards daily and spend every spare moment fantasising about winning so you can quit your job?

- Hide in the office loos for a good cry twice a day?

- Go into kamikaze Facebook mode and post triumphant daily

missives on your wall about how no one notices that you turn up an hour late and do *nothing* all day?

- Genuinely consider throwing yourself under a bus or train on the way in to work?

If any of the above apply, you should *definitely* consider a change in your career. However, if your complaints are more of this variety:

- I don't feel completely fulfilled by my job.

- I am not being as creative as I would like to be.

- My Christmas bonus wasn't big enough to pay for the loft conversion.

- I don't feel as though I am valued sufficiently for the work I do.

- The espresso machine makes *very* poor quality coffee.

- I *only* get thirty days' paid holiday each year.

Then consider that what needs changing or adjusting is probably your expectations. And your attitude. A job is still a job, even the glamorous ones or those you envy. The person whose job it is to play with puppies all day at Battersea Dogs' Home (I've no idea if this is a real job) has to clean up dog shit. Ryan Gosling's masseuse still has to deal with fat, hairy old men. Actually, scotch that, she still has my dream job. That guy who got the job looking after the idyllic desert island had to manage without human interaction and WiFi. *Nothing is going to make you feel entirely fulfilled.* You choose how you feel about stuff. Period. So maybe it is time to make friends with the fact that you have a pretty amazing job already, that your boss is not in fact a total arsehole, that you are paid well and treated with respect, and that the work plays to *some* of your strengths. No job will play to them all. No job alone is going to make you 'happy'.

THE GRIT DOCTOR SAYS:

Either CHOOSE the job you have or CHOOSE to do something else and set about making it happen without further ado.

PROFESSIONAL BUMS

Not everyone is interested in a career. There are some for whom the idea of a career is totally overrated. Fair enough. If you would rather do something fairly mindless so you can turn up in any state and complete your day zombiefied, great. This requires a different sort of pluck, but no more and no less than for you career-crazed types. And neither is better or worse, for that matter. Whatever *works* for you, works for me: if that means partying like a rock star, or travelling the world for six months on a shoestring and then nailing back-to-back night shifts in a crisp factory for six months, go for it. There is nothing wrong with not having ambitions in the job arena.

Grit Doctor caveat: Do whatever it is that you are doing to the best of your ability, so that you feel good about yourself when your day is done: no skiving and no slacking. Your day will pass by much more quickly (which surely must be the aim) if you are fully absorbed in what you are doing. And keep your eye on the prize, be that a pay-rise, your next trip to India or a binge at Bestival.

THE GRIT DOCTOR SAYS:

No whingeing and no complaining about your job. YOU CHOSE IT and if you are not happy with it then *do something about it*. If someone has told you that it is all you are good for or capable of, stop letting this hold you back. It is a story. IT IS BULLSHIT. Our only limits are those we artificially place upon ourselves.

10

HAVING IT ALL

'Having it all' is of course a phrase coined by Shirley Conran and beloved of women's magazines and the *Daily Mail* – generally in articles designed to make women feel bad about themselves. It is an expression I would have BANNED. 'Having it all' has created a monstrous burden for all working mothers, who end up 'doing it all' or 'managing it all' and most certainly being *responsible for it all*. It turns Green Grass Thinking into a pandemic and has us all feeling as though what we have is not enough, is never going to be enough, that we are in fact not good enough, not pretty, thin or clever enough, *not enough*. It panders to women's desire to be everything to everyone all of the time and not to care a jot about themselves.

The truth is that there is *no such effing thing as having it all*. It immediately fails the opportunity cost test, which states that in every choice between two things there has to be loss – the loss of the next best alternative. Every choice involves a sacrifice: choosing involves losing, remember? So, in the context of the 'having it all' debate, the idea that a woman is having it all by working full time and raising her babies is a fallacy. One of those jobs has to be outsourced – temporarily perhaps, or part time – but *outsourced* nonetheless. There is work, there is childcare, and there may be all sorts of domestic arrangements in place to help out with all this, but there is never either:

a) A woman teaching A level English while breastfeeding her twins

or

b) A woman pushing her toddler on the swings while performing open heart surgery.

THE GRIT DOCTOR SAYS:

Having it all is a misnomer.

We need a shift in focus, away from *having it all* and towards *giving our all*. Not just in a charitable sense, but in the sense of giving ourselves completely to whatever it is that we are doing. Because, ultimately, that is what will really make a difference, to our own lives, and the lives of others, while giving us back our mojo. It is time to take stock, and give thanks for everything we do have. It may be boring and old-fashioned to say it but we never have to look very far to find someone with a hell of a lot less. We spend an awful lot of time trapped in GGT, always looking to those who we think have more than us, and precious little time thinking of those in much worse circumstances than ourselves. There are billions of people who will live their entire lives outside of our privileged zone, without access to food, let alone the luxury of coveting their neighbour's possessions, and we would do well to remember them more often. Not because it is saintly, but because it lends fresh perspective to our own lives, and can help inspire and motivate us to do something about it.

Ruth

We have just had our bathroom done. Everything that could go wrong did go wrong. The plumber had been booked over a weekend while I was away with the twins because there would be no running water, but delivery was delayed, then the cistern of the new toilet was broken, the sink was chipped, the shower door warped — all sorts of problems. But I stuck to my plan of returning on the Tuesday, despite the fact that we still had no running water. We arrived to utter chaos.

Anyway, the next day I dropped the twins off at the childminder's and came home to find the plumber upstairs, busy working. I introduced myself in a Grit Doctorly fashion, trying to convey through my tone of voice the urgency of the situation and my dismay at the delays. The plumber — a lovely Albanian guy — had arrived at the crack of dawn and hadn't left the bathroom since. Whenever I went up to offer him a cuppa, he refused me, so absorbed was he in his work and so polite he obviously didn't want to be any trouble. Eventually he told me he was also a twin. I promptly replied that his mother must be a saint (feeling like one myself). He looked up at me with a confused expression: there were six other children in his family, they were born and raised in a communist dictatorship where they had precious little to eat and two sheep to feed a family of ten. His father worked twelve-hour night shifts and his mother had to make eight-hour round trips to get food and collect milk prescriptions ON FOOT.

God, how embarrassing. I meekly offered him a biscuit, which he refused with a smile and got back to work immediately. He was the most polite, smiley, softly spoken man. Once I got over feeling so embarrassed, I was humbled and inspired by his tale. Inspired to stop whingeing incessantly about my middle-class building issues and start giving thanks and appreciating the fact that I didn't have to walk for four hours to get a prescription for milk for the twins. Yes, they are annoying, and yes, it is a huge inconvenience having no bathroom, but what has happened to your context and perspective please, Ruth?

I have no idea, really, about True Grit because I live in Muswell Hill and the full extent of my worries is getting time to escape from the babies so that I can dream up ideas for books and squeezing in a run in the woods. I made a mental note to myself to stop being such a DICK and start worrying about the bigger picture and trying to take action to really make a difference in the short time I have on this earth. I had been boring myself with my cynicism and whingeing and worrying, and I realised through listening to the plumber that happiness, joy, contentment – like all states of mind – is ultimately a choice. That it doesn't happen TO US. We happen to it. We choose our mood.

THE GRIT DOCTOR INSTRUCTS:

Let's replace HAVING it all with GIVING our all, BEING our all.

GYST is all about doing what you choose to do to the best of your ability. Accepting that there is loss involved in every choice between things. We have to suck it up. Life is hard. It is meant to be hard. The magic is in the hard. Hard is the new black, remember?

But this doesn't mean being a martyr and living in a state of permanent self-sacrifice, either: giving everything away so that you are left with nothing. It means *giving all that you are to the task at hand*, to your job – be that at home with the kids or teaching in a school or caring for a sick relative – and to your life. Not so that you are always feeling overwhelmed by 'home' and 'job', but by tackling it *one shelf at a time*. All the time. It is about cleaning that 'shelf' so thoroughly and being so present to the process that you finally see that bit of rotten woodwork underneath the marmalade and are willing to fix it at last. When you have finished, that shelf is looking the best it can possibly look, everything resting upon it is meant to be there and is in some kind of recognisable order so you can access it with the minimum amount of effort and fuss, and nothing is rotting or wasting away.

THE GRIT DOCTOR SAYS:

THE SHELF IS YOUR LIFE. When we start to take action – relevant and pertinent action – we call forth WHO WE REALLY ARE.

Ruth

A word of advice for new mums . . .

Take it as read that all new mums feel like shit, are insecure, don't have a clue what they are doing and need bigging up. As a new mum yourself, assume that all other new mums are starved of sleep and food and paranoid beyond belief. They may be looking at you and thinking you have got your shit together because you made it to playgroup with make-up on and without flecks of shit on your cheek. Through their twitching eyelids and heavy meds, you may seem totally together. Please disabuse them of this delusion at the first available opportunity. The fact that motherhood is shit 90 per cent of the time is really funny. No one needs a good laugh more than a new mum — feck knows I do. What I don't need are fake conversations along the lines of: 'How are you finding it?' 'Yeah, great! She sleeps through from seven till seven, she's a really good baby. We are sooooo lucky.' (Probably code for: 'I went back to work when she was three months old to avoid the almost certain outcome of smashing her head against the wall because she had colic and was driving me insane.')

I was at my god-daughter's baptism on Saturday and Olly offered to keep the twins at home so I could go on my own, which was heavenly. When asked by one of the mums at the christening what it was like having twin toddlers, I said: 'It is awful. Today is the best day I've had in the last two years because they are not with me.' Great ice breaker. Yes it's an exaggeration, but it immediately put the other mother at ease and giggling and open to sharing something funny and dark about her experience. Motherhood takes you to some very dark places and I, for one, find the best way to deal with this is to laugh about it. By the end of lunch I felt totally connected to the three mums there because we had all shown how vulnerable we are by telling the truth, the dark truth, and laughing about it.

Some dark truths about motherhood – ONE of which is my own:

- My pubes have turned grey
- I feel as though I have been sold into slavery
- I don't love my baby as much as I thought I would
- The idea of having sex again makes me want to kill myself – and my husband.

Add your own one-liners to the list above, or borrow one of these, and commit it to memory. Share it with next new mum you meet – guaranteed to give you both a good laugh.

LOVE

Once you have embraced the *love thy neighbour* commandment, and have made friends with your local community, and are smiling a bit more (even through gritted teeth), and are being considerate to others, in a job you have *chosen*, in a clean house feng-shuitted to death (and fit as a fiddle – read *Run Fat B!tch Run* if not) . . . **if you are single and want more than life itself not to be, NOW is the time to get cracking on this one.** This is an area to address once you have got the rest of your shit together, because it is the icing on the cake. The cake itself is the job you are satisfied with, the home that is in order, and the you that is happy in your own skin and able to get through the day without whingeing and complaining and blaming others and circumstances for your life being a certain way. You are in a very strong position now to make a much better choice of partner and will be infinitely more attractive when you know what you are doing with your life. This area – LOVE – is where I did the most work in terms of self-grittification, and I am going to share with you some gritty home truths that I had to suck up:

1. *It was my fault that I was single.* Finding someone to love has to be one of the easiest, most natural and *ordinary* things a human being can do. If you are single and do not want to be, take responsibility for it.

2. *My criteria for a potential partner were narrowing the field into a barely visible blade of grass.* If you have a list with criteria/qualities that potential suitors must possess to stand a chance with you, have a ceremonial burning session of it. If it is all in your head, imagine The Grit Doctor climbing inside your brain and exorcising the list. Criteria/qualities include height, weight, baldness, colour, as well as personality traits and all the other superficial stuff we can get a bit OCD about.

3. *I was too judgemental and failed to give people a chance.* Giving

everyone a chance is not to be translated as sleeping with anyone who offers or committing to a relationship with someone you don't actually like that much. What it does mean is that dweeb from IT who always hovers around you at the Christmas party and who you never give the time of day to – this year, get over yourself and talk to him. It may surprise you.

THE GRIT DOCTOR SAYS:

STOP judging other people and start being a harsher critic of yourself.

---

4. *I had too many rules governing my choices.* One was that I never wanted to marry a criminal barrister. My sister talked me out of this after doing work experience in my chambers and rightly pointing out how lovely some of the guys there were. She persuaded me to give up the rule. I met my husband weeks later, after nearly ten years practising in chambers only a few hundred yards away from each other.

5. *I was in love with a man who would never love me back.* We are only truly single when we are free to fall in love and we are not free until we let go of our pasts/fantasy husband. In my case, I wasted a decade of my life (my 'best years' as my mother always helpfully pointed out) in love with my best friend, who

didn't love me back. I spent all my free time with him and when I wasn't with him, I was mooning over him and so shut out the possibility of meeting somebody else. This is why it is so dangerous. You may think you are single, but if you are in love with someone who doesn't love you back, your heart is already taken and so you are not free to be with anyone else.

THE GRIT DOCTOR WILL SEE YOU NOW

Q: But how do I stop being in love with this fantasy husband/best friend/boss/inappropriate other?

A: The only way to stop the fantasy is to:

1. See whether or not it has any legs **by telling him the truth face to face**; that you love him and have done so for however long;

2. Consider any response short of an immediate declaration of undying love and/or a proposal of marriage to be an outright rejection;

3. **Accept the rejection gracefully** (by which I mean appear graceful);

4. Maintaining graceful demeanour, exit the café/bar/dinner table/bed?!/train immediately (don't thrown yourself off a moving train, wait until the next stop);

5. When safely extricated, behave as disgracefully as your levels of pain and humiliation demand, for as short a time as possible (a weekend is ideal; a fortnight, acceptable; but six months is not);

6. Sober up. Smile. Move on. You are free.

The area of love is where 'the magic' needs to be allowed to operate freely: random encounters and opportunities and giving people a chance – none of it happens until we are open to it. Love has to find you and it can't even *see* you if you have a million walls separating you from it, and a fantasy husband that you are forever mooning over in your spare time. This is one area where you don't get to choose. Love chooses you. It is a gift that we can't rationalise or decide about or create. But we can ensure we never experience it through adopting an attitude that blinds us and twists it out of view.

And there is something truly magical about sharing your life with someone else. Really that is all it is when stripped down to its bare essentials. *Sharing your life with someone.* Not to be underestimated and a good thing to remember when we are fed up, cross and bored and irritated with that person. Not to be confused with deluding ourselves that this position is any better than being single. I was single for a lot longer than most of my contemporaries, who all got married and had kids before I did. And they all felt sorry for me – their single friend. Now I am on the other side of the fence (with them), I am just hugely relieved, not that I got married, but that I was single and lived independently without the enormous responsibilities of marriage and motherhood for as many years as I could get away with it.

COMMITMENT

This is the real biggie. The word makes us all panic slightly. But we all need to make friends with commitment if we want to stand a chance of being in GYSTful swing. Because we spend so much time in between worlds, in between decisions, in between 'stuff', and half-heartedly going for something – so that when we fail we can tell ourselves that it doesn't really matter because we didn't really try anyway. All this attitude does is to resign us to a half-baked kind of life, a life in which we are never actually testing our mettle properly. Do you think Jessica Ennis could have won gold at the Olympics if she'd spent even one day of her life trapped in this mode of thinking? No, of course not. Mo Farah? No chance. We only ever get to where we want to go and achieve our potential when we start to really go for things, and the first step towards really going for things lies in that one simple word: COMMIT-MENT. Being committed is the key to GYST because it takes us out of half-baked mode and shifts us into full-throttle.

Commitment lies at the heart of *every success*. Anything worth aspiring to – in our work, in love, in relationships, the whole she-bang. All successes *and* all big failures have commitment behind them. Failure is every bit as necessary to a good life as success and not necessarily as a stepping-stone either. Just failure as failure without the dressing up. A grit aficionado is someone who sucks up failure with aplomb. Commit to your failures every bit as much as to your successes. Because in committing to your life you don't get to pick and choose the outcomes, whether you win or lose, so go for all of it.

THE GRIT DOCTOR SAYS:

FAILURE. GRIT. Roll those words around in your mouth for a while until you can taste them without feeling sick.

THE GRIT DOCTOR WILL SEE YOU NOW

Q: But what, exactly, is commitment?

A: Commitment is simply a position which says I'M 100 PER CENT IN AND WILL SEE THIS THROUGH NO MATTER WHAT. Commitment provides the framework within which the action to take becomes apparent and makes sense and can be driven through – with verve. So, for example, I am making a commitment to getting my house shipshape! I am committing myself to it. Which takes it from being, 'I'll do it someday if I can be bothered', to being committed to making it happen now. Commitment is the fuel to action's engine. Commitments can be massive or they can be small, but they are always the essence of GYST because making a commitment compels us to take the relevant action. NOW.

DECLARE YOUR COMMITMENTS

Make a commitment to changing something or creating something in your life that you have been thinking about but never got around to doing. Make the commitment to yourself. I AM GOING TO FIND SOMEONE TO SHARE MY LIFE WITH or I AM GOING TO GET PROMOTED. Whatever it is that you have been thinking about a lot, but wavering over in terms of action. Declare it to yourself OUT LOUD. Voice it, make it real, get it out of your head and crucially, out of the pre-shelf phase and drill it into your life. Then start adding the flesh to its bones.

But how? By taking actions consistent with the commitment/declaration you made. Use the GYST Facilitator table on page 47 to help you if necessary. And time-bind it. Using the example of finding someone to share your life with, begin by having an honest conversation with yourself about what actions you have been taking in this regard and whether or not they are consistent with the outcome you desire. Ask yourself, is shagging anything that moves on a Friday night when off your face in a club consistent with finding someone to share your life with? Or is mooning after someone who doesn't love you back during all your spare time consistent with finding someone to share your life with? Using the work example, is turning up to work late every day looking shambolic consistent with getting promoted? Of course not, so start making the necessary adjustments – be they small tweaks or seismic shifts in your behaviour – and start taking the appropriate actions. Use your common sense.

In the first example, that might mean getting friends to arrange blind dates for you or to organise a dinner party for singles; it could mean joining an appropriate singles website, or a club. Maybe you could join forces with a single pal of the opposite sex and go out together to meet interesting other singles. In fact, is this single person who has been a great friend for so many years an appropriate candidate to play the role of love of your life? Are you sure he isn't? Try him out first (translate this as you will) before you write him off completely.

THE GRIT DOCTOR SAYS:

It is a lack of commitment that ensures our shit remains all over the place.

THE GRIT DOCTOR WILL SEE YOU NOW

Q: But what does commitment look like in practice?

A: It looks like this: Andy Murray has recently won the US Open. That win is a great example of his commitment to winning a Grand Slam. Since the age of four, so for the last twenty-one years, he has been taking action consistent with his commitment to winning a Grand Slam: getting up and getting on to the court and hitting balls around until he is exhausted. And when he loses, he just resets the parameters to make them consistent with his commit-ment. His body was not athletic enough so he transformed it. How? Action, action, action. His mind was not strong enough so he worked hard at improving his attitude, his temper, his whole personality on the court – action after action after action, every day, to stay true to his commitment to winning a Grand Slam. In honouring a commitment there are inevitably massive losses. He kept losing in the quarters, the semis and then the finals. He responded by picking himself up and getting back onto the court, never wavering in his commitment, even when his mind was against him, or his body – all that stuff we might blame on our genes. Not Murray. He just kept going until finally the job was done. And his reaction to winning was so telling: relief. Because commitments are not about fanfare and wild applause. **Honouring our commitments is actually just being who we are.**

Making and breaking commitments is very easy to do: 'For better for worse, for richer for poorer' only to end in the divorce courts; 'I'll build the shelves after the footie' only for them to stay in the box for another six months. But breaking these commitments, essentially promises to ourselves and to others, is incredibly damaging to our psychological wellbeing and self-esteem.

This is where your Inner Bitch comes in. She is allergic to commitment breaking – it brings her out in hives and a mild form of Tourette's, which is why when we fail to honour our commitments we feel so awful. The failure to each other is entirely secondary to the failure to ourselves, and to our IBs. We feel shit about ourselves because we have quite literally poisoned our IBs with commitment failure.

Good news: your IB also provides the antidote to commitment troubles: when she is nagging you to finish that task and get those bloody shelves built and not to sit back down in front of the telly, for the love of God DO AS SHE TELLS YOU. This feeds her with the good stuff, makes her happy and energised, and so *you* feel good because you are no longer at loggerheads with her. When you and your IB are in conflict, you are at your most ineffectual and weak, paralysed by the guilt and anxiety that the conflict has generated. And so what happens? The silencers: chocolate, vino, and the lies to yourself about how it doesn't matter, she won't notice, you'll do it tomorrow.

Once you have committed to doing something, even a small task like doing the washing up before bedtime (and it is good to practise with the small stuff), the time to summon your Inner Bitch is *just at the last moment*, before you run out of time. This moment is when she is at the height of her powers. She will scream at you to get the thing done – she is the feeling of increasing anxiety as the deadline approaches, the racing in your pulse, the buzzing in your ear. Being accountable to your Inner Bitch can really work wonders here.

THE GRIT DOCTOR SAYS:

Anything that can be done today, MUST BE DONE TODAY. This is a habit really worth taking on. There will always be unexpected extra shit to deal with tomorrow, as well as the leftover shit you have carried over from the day before, all of which tends to ensure you tackle even less ... thus setting up the vicious cycle once again.

HAPPINESS

Happiness is overrated. It is not some perfect state to which we should aspire. It is just a feeling, as banal and meaningless as all the others that pass through us on a daily basis. The reason we are so unhappy is because we think we are supposed to be happy. We cannot *be* happy. We can only *feel* happy. And feelings are transient – they are fleeting and passing and not to be held on to at the expense of everything else. In scrabbling around for happiness we actually lose out on those moments of pure unbridled joy because we are not present to them. Give up trying to be happy – not just all the time, but *any* of the time. A good life is full of the entire spectrum of human emotion, all the bad and dark and miserable stuff, the failures and the brutal disappointments, every bit as much as the 'happy' stuff. Start choosing to enjoy the dark stuff as much as the happy stuff. This is the key – not looking for silver linings all the time, but cultivating an attitude that allows you to embrace the crappy bits too. We may as well, as there is a whole lot more of it to endure during the course of one's life.

Embracing the dark side can provide an enormous amount of fuel for your motivation tank. Anger, in particular, can be the most powerful of Grit Grenades when channelled cleverly. Crucially, whatever we are feeling, we must never allow it to interfere with the action we are taking or intending to take. We get into difficulty when we choose to cling on to feelings and allow them to dictate whether or not we get our shit together.

If we accept that we have a choice and that we are in charge, why don't we start to exercise our choices more powerfully? Because if you wait to 'feel' like sorting your shit out, you will be waiting most probably for the rest of your life. We have to choose to take action, and to do the right thing, no matter what we are feeling.

'Happiness is not a goal; it is a by-product of a life well lived.' *Eleanor Roosevelt*

LAUGHTER IS THE BEST MEDICINE

Laughter is a powerful antidote to stress, pain and conflict. Nothing is as immediate and effective at bringing our bodies and minds back into balance as a good laugh. Humour lightens our burdens, eases anxiety and fear, relieves stress, improves mood and enhances resilience (the ability to withstand GRIT). Laughter inspires others, generates hope, connects us, and keeps us grounded, focused and alert. It boosts our immune systems, decreases pain, relaxes muscles and prevents heart disease. It defuses arguments and attracts others to us like a magnet. With so much power to heal and renew, the ability to laugh easily and frequently is a tremendous resource at our immediate disposal for surmounting problems, de-escalating conflict, enhancing relationships, and supporting both physical and emotional health. And it is free.

THE GRIT DOCTOR SAYS:

Stop associating laughter with happiness. They are not connected in any way.

EXERCISE: LAUGH YOUR WAY INTO ACTION

It's belly laughs we are after, the full-on guffaw brought about by hilarious slapstick comedy or my rapier wit. Not a polite little 'teehee' but laughing till it hurts. Commit to your laughter as much as to your life. Full out: 100 per cent.

THE GRIT DOCTOR SAYS:

HahahahahahahahaHAHAHAHHAHAHHAHAHAHAHH AHAHHHHAHAHA!!!!!!

THE FINAL WORD

MAKING FRIENDS WITH DEATH

What better way to finish a book than with a quick nod to where we all end up: dead. This is the real biggie that we all avoid thinking about and talking about at any cost. We can't even say it – DEAD – when offering our condolences to friends. Instead, we skirt around the issue, calling it a 'loss' (as if the person can subsequently be found) or a 'passing' on, or any number of other words and phrases that fail to stand up to scrutiny. We cannot bear to say, 'I am so sorry that your dad died'. What is so awful about that? We have become so afraid of death that we go to extraordinary lengths to avoid mention of its name, even at funerals. This is, quite frankly, a ridiculous state of affairs.

> 'It is not sad to die. The sad thing is not to live intensely while you are alive.' *Albert Espinosa*

Death is where we are all headed, death is the thing we cannot avoid, cannot control and that no manner of shit togetherness is going to stop happening. And there is truly eff all we can do about it. In Ireland death is laid out for everyone to see, in a coffin in the living room where family and friends can come and pay their respects. They look death in the face and have a drink with it, which strikes me as a much more positive and realistic approach to the whole thing. I am not here to debate the merits of an afterlife, but I truly believe that in avoiding death we are missing out on a vital component to life: one which paradoxically makes our lives richer, more productive and more fulfilling.

Reflecting upon our mortality once in a while can be incredibly uplifting. This doesn't mean slipping into fantasy mode and pondering your funeral – what will be played and said and how many people will attend – it means remembering that your time on earth is short, that it may come to an end sooner than you think and if it were to happen tomorrow – *your death* – well, what have you got to show for your life so far? This can be the ultimate Grit Grenade and is a brilliant way to help you prioritise, providing you are reasonably sane and responsible. There is nothing like a little bit of death to get me fired up and motivated for life. Just imagine what you would do if you knew you were going to die, say, in six months' time? Where would you live? What job would you be doing? How much sex would you be having? Which places would you visit, what adventures would you have? What would you actually do *right now*?

THE GRIT DOCTOR SAYS:

Pondering your demise once in a while can be incredibly motivating. Death is the new black.

And no, I don't mean live as though each day is your last and be reckless as hell. I mean live your life like it really matters now. Don't live it for some unknown quantity that may or may not happen in the future. Don't live it in the wings, waiting for your real life to begin: when your ducks are lined up, when you are thin, when you are rich, when you have kids, or when your kids have left home! We only have *now* and we don't know how much more 'now' we are going to have. Now. NOW. **NOW. THIS IS IT.** This is the life you have, the one you are living, not the fantasy one in the massive house with staff and a richer husband. This one, in the small house with the demanding kids and the irritating husband who puts up with all your shit and loves you for it. Cherish them all for who they are today, not for what they might become at some date in an uncertain future when everything is better or different in some way. There is no better and different. There is only now. Not leaving things for tomorrow becomes a whole lot easier when you consider that there may not in fact be a tomorrow.

ONE STEP AT A TIME

In *Run Fat B!tch Run*, we learned that stretching those long-forgotten leg muscles once again, and repeating the sometimes painful process over and over and over again, even when you didn't 'feel' like it, strengthened those muscles in a way you had previously not believed possible. You probably didn't know those muscles existed in the first place. We learned through the discipline of running regularly that what we thought was impossible became possible through the simple art of practice, of putting one foot in front of the other.

In exercising those muscles, we realised not only that they were there, but what they were capable of through regular use. You may have been shit at sport at school, you may have always pulled a sicky during PE and convinced yourself over a lifetime that sport of any kind was just not for you – that you couldn't do it, that you had the wrong build, that you were too fat, and all manner of other excuses. And then you chose to give up those excuses. You summoned your Inner Bitch and got gritty with yourself.

The same can be applied to all other muscles. Calf muscles, butt muscles, brain muscle – it can *all* be improved through regular use. Whatever we were born with, we can improve upon it exponentially through discipline and practice: the building blocks of grit. When we feel that we have reached our 'limit', it is only because we have not yet trained our muscles to go further. Using running as an analogy, maybe you trained and managed to run in a 10 km race. And now you want to run a marathon. But you will not be able to – it would be impossible for your leg muscles to see you through until you have trained them to that distance. In other words, the marathon may be the goal but you are going to have to run a hell of a lot of shorter runs, increasing the distance by tiny increments over a long period of time, before you can ever hope to reach the finishing line.

THE GRIT DOCTOR SAYS:

Grit is the greatest gift of all. And is a gift that we give to ourselves. GRIT TURNS GIFTS INTO GOLD.

It is the same with everything in life. A clean home cannot be achieved overnight, but through tackling it one shelf at a time it will be transformed. A new career will not happen in a day, but in identifying what it is that you want to do, and committing to it – shelf by shelf – it will. We may not be Mandelas yet, with our minds fully focused on justice and equality for all, but by starting to smile at our neighbours, engaging fully, listening and speaking carefully, exercising fairness and kindness in all our dealings with others, the ripples will be felt. A tidal wave begins with a tiny ripple just as a tidy home begins with one clean shelf. And it is all the same. A revolution begins with taking a stand. Holding hands with your Inner Bitch, scrubbing brush in hand and starting on that kitchen cupboard shelf, I dare you, no, I double dare you to change the world.

'What can you do to promote world peace?
Go home and love your family.' *Mother Teresa*

If you take on only one thing from this book let it be this:

BE
IN
ACTION

Embrace these three words and watch how your shit starts to shape up. OK, bitches? Let's get doing.

'I'm not talking about blind optimism, the kind of hope that just ignores the enormity of the tasks ahead or the road blocks that stand in our path. I'm not talking about the wishful idealism that allows us to just sit on the side-lines or shirk from a fight. I have always believed that hope is that stubborn thing inside us that insists, despite all the evidence to the contrary, that something better awaits us so long as we have the courage to keep reaching, to keep working, to keep fighting.'

Barack Obama's re-election speech in Chicago, 2012

He is talking about GRIT.

GLOSSARY

G my ST: Get my Shit Together

Grinstinct: Smile, grit your teeth and JUST DO

Grit Doctor it: Turn it on its head, make it harder

Grit dodger: Those who are allergic to grit

Grit fiends: Those to whom grit cometh easy

Grit it out: Clench those teeth and push on through to the other side

Gritgasm: The incredible climactic feeling of having finally Feng Shuitted your entire home

Gritmin: Admin, which we all know to be deathly boring

Grittification: The application of grit to all aspects of your life

Grittify: Make grittier

GYST: Get your shit together

GYSTful: A get-your-shit-together way to approach a problem

unGYSTful: Totally lacking in all forms of grit; glued to sofa and remote control

If you've been inspired to **Get Your Sh!t Together**,

get in touch and let us know about it . . .

Twitter

@gritdoctor

#gyst

Facebook

www.facebook.com/thegritdoctor

The Grit Doctor's Blog

www.gritdoctor.com

RUN FAT B!TCH RUN
by Ruth Field

IT'S TIME TO GIVE THOSE SKINNY B!TCHES A RUN FOR THEIR MONEY

Is there a large arse-shaped dent in your sofa? An eye-wateringly expensive (and rarely used) gym membership burning a hole in your bank account? Does the sight of your wobbly thighs leave you cowering under the duvet?

Then it's time you faced the truth: the only option is to lace up trainers and hit the ground running.

Straight-talking, funny and brutally honest, **RUN FAT B!TCH RUN** will give you – yes, you – the push you need to get out of the door, pounding the pavements and shedding pounds in no time.

Hate running? No worries. **RUN FAT B!TCH RUN** will give you all the tools you need to transform that passion into real motivation.

Locate your **inner grit** and long-lost energy

Follow a fuss-free and completely **foolproof** beginners' programme

Throw away the scales, stock up on pasta and enjoy **carbs without guilt**

Amusingly vicious . . . Excellent advice all round.
Emma Thompson

If you're stuck in an exercise rut, this book will give you a rather rude kick up the backside . . . it certainly shamed us into lacing up our Nikes!
Closer

A witty, no-nonsense read, it had us dusting off our trainers within seconds. Trust us when we say you'll be up and running in no time at all.
Grazia

Ruth is an inspiring running-buddy . . . By the time I unpack my summer wardrobe, I'm sure my inner Grit Doctor will be my best friend.
Flic Everett, *Daily Express*

THE RUN FAT B!TCH RUN MARATHON PLAN

Motivation, Training, Nutrition: The Grit Doctor Way

by Ruth Field

Ebook exclusive

The marathon . . . a word to strike fear into the hearts of all weekend runners; a challenge like no other; *a hell of a long way*.

And you've just signed up. Bugger.

But never fear, you are not alone. The Grit Doctor is back with a vengeance and she's determined to whip you into shape. With THE RUN FAT B!TCH RUN MARATHON PLAN you'll . . .

Find the **MOTIVATION** to transform yourself from casual jogger to elite(ish) athlete

Create simple **TRAINING** plans to help you increase distance, stamina and speed

Cook fuss-free, tasty food which will provide all the **NUTRITION** your aching body needs

26 miles? BRING IT ON.

Plus: race-day strategies, useful resources, fundraising tips and plenty of The Grit Doctor's trademark honesty, humour and tough love.

26 REASONS TO RUN

by Ruth Field and
The Run Fat B!tch Runners

Free ebook exclusive

*I wouldn't go to my husband's Christmas party because I had nothing to wear that fitted me and refused to buy anything. I vowed that night that I would shift the excess weight. It was shortly after this that I read **Run Fat B!tch Run** – and it has changed my life around completely. Now five-and-a-half stone lighter I am now training to compete in The Dublin Marathon in October of this year.*

Are you suffering from **Motivation Meltdown**? Have your well-worn-in trainers lain dormant for a few months, or are you simply looking for that first push to **get up**, **lace up** and **RUN**?

Then look no further, for here are the stories from 26 women who have been exactly where you are (on the sofa, right?) and fought back . . . with a little help from **The Grit Doctor**. Their stories are all here to give you a **Motivation Marathon** every time you're tempted to give up and give in to the takeaway menu.

Funny, moving and incredibly inspiring, each of these women found their own reasons to get running and beat the bulge – and so can you.

sphere

To buy any of our books and to find out
more about Sphere and Little, Brown Book Group,
our authors and titles, as well as events and
book clubs, visit our website

www.littlebrown.co.uk

and follow us on Twitter

@LittleBrownUK

To order any Sphere titles p & p free in the UK,
please contact our mail order supplier on:

+ 44 (0)1832 737525

Customers not based in the UK should contact
the same number for appropriate postage
and packing costs.